Dear Earl,

We hope you [...]
this little book. It go[...]
reviews, but unfortunately i[...]
out-of-print. Hold on to it —
I may need to borrow it in a few
years! Fondly,

How to Be
the Perfect
Mother-in-Law

How to Be the Perfect *Mother-in-Law*

CAMILLE RUSSO
with
MICHAEL SHAIN

Andrews and McMeel
A Universal Press Syndicate Company
Kansas City

Library of Congress Cataloging-in-Publication Data
Russo, Camille.
    How to be the perfect mother-in-law /
    Camille Russo with Michael Shain.
        p. cm.
        1. Mothers-in-law — Family relationships — Handbooks,
manuals, etc.   2. Family — Handbooks, manuals, etc.
I. Russo, Camille.   II. Shain, Michael, 1949–.   III. Title.
HQ759.25.R87 1997
646.7'8 — dc2   96-52850
                                                                CIP

To my father, Joseph,
who made sure I learned how to type,
and my mother, Virginia,
who taught me how to care.

Contents

Acknowledgments

I WISH TO THANK all the people who shared their experiences, their common sense, and their hearts with me: my nieces Virginia Stanco and Kim Roggeman, Eileen Cespuglio, Dr. Lorraine Ronca, Dr. Catherine Tayag, Tommy Tracy, Linda Heidinger, Rene Feduniue, my mother-in-law Elaine Shain, Louise Curry, and, as always, Jeannete Russo, who taught me how to be.

Thank-you to those who made sure my words said what I meant: Brian McDonald, Pat Brennan, Walter Wager, Frank DeCaro, Maria Fernandez, Jean Zevnik, and Michael Corriero.

My thanks to Elaine Kaufman, whose advice got me over the rough spots, and Ruth Heidinger, a very special friend.

I am grateful to Al Vitarelli; he made sure I got to where I had to go.

I want to thank my clients for their patience and trust.

Thank-you to my brave agent, Jane Dystel, who put her faith in a first-timer, and to my editor Christine Schillig, who figured out how to make sense of my nonsense without taking away my voice.

Thank-you to John Lombardi, my son and colleague, who makes me laugh at myself and spent endless months making sure I got this book right.

Thank-you to my beautiful, extraordinary daughter-in-law Mary Lombardi, who helped me to understand how special our relationship can be and then allowed me to share it with others.

Thank-you to my sisters, Anna, Catherine, and Ruthie: Your love kept me going.

And thank-you especially to my best friend, Frank Heidinger, who first suggested I write a book and then encouraged me the entire way. If you don't like this book, blame him.

Finally, thank-you to my brother Andrew. Because you loved to read, I learned how to write.

Introduction

OR THE LAST thirty-five years, I've been somebody's daughter-in-law. In all, I've had three mothers-in-law. If you want to know what qualifies a person to write a book called *How to Be the Perfect Mother-in-Law,* I think having three mothers-in-law says it all.

But the idea for this book didn't start there. It grew out of my practice as a relationship therapist. The problems I deal with most of the time are with people who are constantly second-guessing themselves in their relationships and wondering how they should handle difficult family situations. They don't know "how to be." Some don't know how to be good girlfriends or wives. Others really don't know how to be good stepparents. But the hardest relationship of all, it seems, is how to be a good mother-in-law.

By the time they come to me, these frustrated mothers-in-law want to bang their heads against the wall. They don't have a clue how they got into so much trouble with their in-law children.

At first, I could not understand why they were having such a hard time. They had good jobs and careers. They'd raised huge families. They'd raised huge families and gone back to graduate school *at the same time*. But they were ready to throw themselves out the window because they could not figure out how to get along with their married children.

"You never had a problem with any of your mothers-in-law?" they would ask.

Not really. After three mothers-in-law, why had I never had an unpleasant word with any of them? It may have been the two rules I followed faithfully. I never complained to them about their sons and I always told them their sons were the best. Is there anything else a mother wants to hear about her child? Of course not.

I was sure I had the daughter-in-law thing down pat. Or maybe I'd just been blessed with three good mothers-in-law. One way or another, it never bothered me much because my relationships with my mothers-in-law had been great.

Then, a few years ago, my own son got married and the question became frighteningly real. What should I do to be a good mother-in-law? That's how this book began. I wanted to help my clients untangle themselves from the messes they were in and find some peace with their in-law children. And I helped myself at the same time.

As the youngest of four children, I had an excellent role model. I watched my mother handle the demands of being a daughter-in-law *and* a mother-in-law for many years. My father was the oldest of 10 children and my grandmother's favorite. In her eyes, my father could do no wrong. My mother knew different, but she never once let her mother-in-law know that she didn't share her opinion.

With her in-law children, my mother had her own set of rules. She treated them like her own—at times making us feel as if *we* were the in-laws. They got the best of everything at her house. She fussed over them more than us, deferred to them more than to us, and fed them more than us. At times, it drove us crazy, but I always knew what she was up to. She loved us and we knew it. She wanted her in-law children to know she cared for them too.

And it worked. She convinced each one that he or she was secretly her favorite. Whether still married or divorced, all her in-law children loved my mother to death.

My other role model is Rose Lombardi, my first mother-in-law. She taught me an equally valuable lesson. As a very pregnant nineteen-year-old, I was out with my husband one night and in a very good mood. In my happy state, I lost my mind, thought I was Julia Child, and invited some very important people over for dinner. Actually, I didn't just invite these people. I *insisted* that they come—a brave and foolish thing to do, because in those days I didn't know how to boil an egg.

The day before the dinner, I was in a panic. My mother lived too far away to give me a hand. I couldn't afford take-out; we didn't have that kind of money. I knew I was dead.

That's when my mother-in-law dropped by. Realizing the mess I'd gotten myself into, Rose told me to relax and get a cake and a couple of bottles of red wine. She'd handle the rest.

The next day was a scorcher—something like 98 degrees. But there was Rose pulling her shopping cart into our apartment. She took out a big pot of spaghetti sauce, a Tupperware container full of meatballs, and two roasted chickens wrapped tightly in aluminum foil. I just stood there as she set everything on the stove. She laid out linens and plates on the dining room table; she even filled my coffeepot. Then, as she turned to leave, she made me swear I would not tell anyone —including her son—about her help.

The night was a huge success. No one at the dinner ever knew what I'd done (or, actually, hadn't done). And since I never told him, I assume Joey, my first husband, is learning about this for the first time too. To those people who came to dinner at my house in August 1963, I confess: I took all the credit, but I didn't cook a thing.

I was too young to fully appreciate Rose's gift to me that night. Eventually, when I learned to cook, I realize how much shopping and preparation had gone into making me look good. Rose wasn't insulted because she hadn't been invited. She didn't want any credit. She just didn't want to see me fail.

In the pages ahead, if you recognize yourself, don't take it too seriously. So what if you go to your children's house unannounced? Who knew it was a crime? Now you know. If you want to make them happy, you'll call ahead. This isn't brain surgery.

And if you should find something of your in-law children in here, don't take that too seriously either. They won't bring back the death penalty for daughters-in-law who forget to call every week. Relax. You're both just learning how to be.

1

Why You Want to Be the Perfect Mother-in-Law

WHEN YOUR CHILD came home that first time with a boyfriend or girlfriend, it was a happy moment for you, I presume. You were ready to welcome him or her into your family with open arms, right? Maybe this was the first time in your married life that a major family decision was completely out of your hands, but you were ready to accept your son or daughter's choice of a mate without a peep.

After they got married, you thought: Here comes the easy part. You would treat your in-law children as your own and everyone would live happily ever after. Wasn't this the start of the best years of your life? Weren't these the good times you'd been waiting for? So why do you feel as if you've been strapped to a chair with a sock stuck in your mouth?

Why is it that everything you say seems to cause trouble with your married children? Why can't you speak up anymore? Can't you defend your own child? Can't you tell your in-law child exactly how you feel? Why shouldn't you want to see them more often? Suddenly, the simple question "How are you?" is no longer a simple expression of caring.

Your married children think you're demanding to see their latest bank statement.

You know every last detail about the lives of the children you have raised, from toilet training to the first broken hearts to the cost of senior-prom night. When did your child *stop* being your business? And who forgot to tell you?

You were a damn good mother, or at least you tried to be. You made some mistakes. We all do. But during the growing-up years, you worked like hell to do the right things for your children and give them everything you possibly could.

What has happened to you since your child said "I do" is something like going through a time warp. I take that back —a role warp. It occurred sometime between the first chords of "The Wedding March" and throwing the rice. You didn't do anything wrong, except maybe pay too much for the reception. Becoming a mother-in-law is not something you do. It's something that happens to you—like cellulite.

For the most part, the family roles we play throughout our lives come with a set of preprogrammed instructions. No one has to tell a little girl how to hug and kiss her father. She knows how to do that; the feelings are built in. No one has to tell a little boy when to defend his mother. A classmate's nasty remark about his mom probably sparked his first playground fight.

Think about it. You've already juggled at least three or four significant family roles. You learned how to go from being a daughter to being a wife, and from a wife to a mother—huge personal changes, really. Weren't you a different kind of mother to your first-born child than you were to your last one? That's another kind of role change. And the job of parenting a two-year-old was vastly different from being the parent of a teenager. These are just a few examples of how you adjusted to the twists and turns of family life.

Now you have a brand-new part to play. No big deal. You did it before, you'll do it again.

If you are a brand-new mother-in-law, these pages will show you how to stay out of trouble. (All right, you're bound to have a *little* trouble now and then, but nothing you can't handle.)

If you're a veteran mother-in-law, these pages will protect you from becoming smug or complacent. Just because you don't do all the annoying things *your* mother-in-law did doesn't mean that you have this mother-in-law thing down pat. Without realizing it, you may be doing a million other annoying mother-in-law things of your own invention.

Somewhere in our hearts and minds is planted the instinct to protect and nurture our children, be loyal to our parents, and strangle our obnoxious little brothers. These are the blood ties and family roles that come to us naturally. The way we feel and act around Mom, Dad, Junior, and Sis is innate.

But there is nothing "natural" about being a mother-in-law. We have no instinctive feelings or genetic code to guide us. In fact, most of our natural responses, like the instinct to shield our children from harm, work *against* the goal of becoming a good mother-in-law. But you can learn to adapt to this new role. Millions have.

So far so good. If you want a good relationship with your child and want to enjoy peace within your family, here are some of the best ways to accomplish that. You can learn what it takes to be a perfect mother-in-law.

Why bother? Simple. To get all those hugs and kisses you deserve from your grandchildren, you must have an untroubled relationship with their mother or father. Have you ever liked anyone who actively fought with your mother or father? Of course not.

I'll give you another good reason. Your daughter-in-law will probably have the final say on which nursing home you'll be sent to. Didn't think of that, did you?

2

Young Love

*T*HERE IS NOTHING quite like first love. Can you remember what it was like? The intensity, the first overwhelming feelings? Not many folks forget it. Some of us spend the rest of our lives trying to recapture it, though I don't know many who do.

In the lives of many mothers, young love is the first thing that happens to their children that they have absolutely no control over. It can be beautiful or it can be devastating. Most of the movies about young love don't show the wear and tear it has on mothers. Maybe it's a Hollywood conspiracy, but in "teenage" movies the mother is always portrayed as a nervous ninny with a high-pitched voice.

As parents, we carry around some pretty strong opinions about what is right for our children. We have firm ideas about when our daughters are old enough to wear makeup or when our sons are mature enough to go out of town with their friends. Most of all, we have strong ideas about when our kids are ready to get married. Sometimes the kids don't share those ideas.

In the endless war between parents and children, once

you say no, your kids will usually figure out how to get around you anyway. They are very good at it, and they should be; they've had years of practice! Think about all the hours they spent in their rooms while growing up, plotting ways to get back at you. By their late teens, most kids are professionals at maneuvering around you.

If you're in a panic that your son or daughter is on the verge of getting married too young, here are some uncomfortable thoughts and practical advice.

No matter how clearly or often you describe all the things that can go wrong when young people marry too soon, your child won't see it the way you do. This isn't a rational or logical discussion. This is about first love, hormone-pounding, palm-sweating, heart-stopping first love. It's about a deep, uncontrollable feeling your child has. And you'll have to let the feeling run its course before your otherwise levelheaded kid returns to his or her senses.

It doesn't help if you've been through it all before with your other children. Maybe this is your second or third brush with young love. It doesn't matter. It will forever be the first time for this child, and young love never loses the power to tip your world upside down.

Your daughter probably has nagging doubts and fears about running off to Michigan with the rock drummer she met two weeks ago. Don't bother to tell her it could be a dumb thing to do. She knows there is nothing she can do about it. She is being driven by feelings that are brand-new to her. It's a shame, but your doubts won't stop her.

One night your son will come home babbling about a girl you may never have set eyes on. Suddenly, her opinion on things becomes vastly more important than yours. He is now impressed with everything she says, thinks, or feels. If she hates the beach and loves the mountains, no matter how many perfect summers your family has spent at the seashore, he's headed for the Rockies come July. If she's a vegetarian, your son will suddenly turn his nose up at steak and then try to convince you that the reason he wouldn't touch vegetables before meeting her was because "you never made them right."

Strangest of all, your child will suddenly start paying attention to all the manners you've tried to teach for years—like being polite, respectful, and attentive. All the stuff you struggled to get your kids to do with the family will become very important. Your son will want you to invite his new girl to all the family affairs. He'll want you to talk to her, put her on your Christmas card list, maybe call her mother now and then just to say hello.

You may end up liking the young person your son or daughter has fallen in love with. Or you may discover you can't bear the sight of the surly, smart-alecky adolescent your child dotes on. Love or hate the kid, it makes no difference, you can't change what has happened. You can't stand in the way of love. It's too powerful. Give in to it, and you might have a chance of rescuing your child from a bad spot. Fight it, and you'll both be washed away.

Cruel as this may sound, it is sometimes best to allow your child to struggle—and suffer—through this experience without your interference. Adding confusion and getting in the way won't change a thing. The only thing you'll accomplish by fighting is to shut down the relationship with your child. Once it's known that you're against the marriage, he or she won't be coming back to you.

So what do you do? In the end, you're left with just one choice: Support your child's decision.

When your son was benched in Little League, you gave the coach a piece of your mind. When your daughter came home from school crying because she wasn't cast in the lead role in *Cinderella*, you sympathized. In other words, you stood behind them no matter what. You two were a united front.

That united front is, in fact, what your son or daughter has begun to form with the new partner. When you try to derail this new relationship, you become that stupid Little League coach or that mean old drama teacher. Your son will wonder, "Doesn't my mother trust me?" When that happens, he begins doubting *your* judgment. "What does my mother know anyway?" your daughter asks. "She doesn't really understand how I feel, probably never did."

For example, your nineteen-year-old comes home from college on spring break with a girl. She's been telling him to drop out of school, find a job, and get an apartment with her. Sometime down the road, he can continue his education, she says. Maybe she already has a child from a previous marriage. Bad news.

This is not what you had wanted for your son — a ready-made family before he ever finishes school. Someone will probably have to strap you to a sturdy chair after you hear what this young woman has planned for him.

So what are you supposed to do, just stand there and let it happen?

Frankly, yes. The last thing in the world you want to do is push him to the moment when he will have to take sides. If you do, chances are the side he chooses will not be yours. He will instinctively jump to her protection; he has to. Don't blame him. It's a natural reaction when you're in love.

Your job is to avoid putting him in the role of hero protector. And you do that by staying out of the middle. The moment you try to show him that he may be making a big mistake, your son is no longer focused on the girl who wants him to drop out of school. All he'll see is *you* picking on *her*. If you insist on making yourself a player in this drama, you can say good-bye to any hope that he will come to his senses in your natural lifetime.

If you can stay out of his relationship (without having a total mental breakdown), he will have a clear sight of her—and the situation he is getting himself into. Remember, stay out of his field of vision so he can see clearly.

Another example: Your young daughter's good-for-nothing fiancé didn't call her at 8 P.M. as he promised. It's about the two-hundredth time he's done this, and your daughter is upset again. You are finally ready to say a few choice words about this man she wants to marry. If you start in about his inconsiderateness, what do you think will happen when he eventually calls at eleven? She will be thrilled to hear from him because she no longer has to look at your sour face or hear you question her judgment. Your nagging has successfully taken her attention off her where-is-he-now boyfriend, whose true feelings she needs to question seriously. Instead, she is focusing her resentment on you. Not what you had in mind, right?

The smart thing for you to do is stop picking on the person your son or daughter wants to marry. If your son is set on a girl who wants him to drop out for her. If your daughter wants some guy who makes her wait three hours every night, what can you do about it? Very little, I'm afraid.

Say nothing, and give your child time to think about what is happening. It's your only hope.

3

Surviving Your Son's Wedding, More or Less

I KNOW THAT WOMEN get a little crazy when it comes to planning a wedding. But I also know that men show an infuriating indifference about wedding plans. Brides and grooms may walk the same aisle together, but they take very different paths getting to the altar.

In most cases, a man avoids getting married for a good part of his life, while a woman dreams about her wedding day from the time she's a little girl. These different expectations can lead to a lot of trouble on the road to "I Do."

I was very lucky with my son, knock on wood. When John told me he was getting married, I was delighted. Though I really didn't know her well, I liked his fiancée, Mary. I could tell she had a good heart and loved my son. That was enough for me.

By the time the wedding was over, I had grown to love my daughter-in-law very much. Her family was close and supportive of one another. I couldn't have asked for better. I didn't have a worry in the world about Mary; it was John I wasn't too crazy about.

During the weeks of planning for the wedding, my son

was giving Mary a rough time. Not on purpose, really. But I could see that she had to ask him ten times for everything she needed him to do. Ten times: Did he call about the limo? Ten times: Did all the ushers know where the tuxedo place was? My son must have heard her with the same ears he had when I asked him to clean up his room or study his math. Mary had replaced me at the top of John's yes-her-to-death-then-pay-her-no-mind list.

Men think that women make a big deal out of everything, just for the sake of making a big deal. I suppose they are right; sometimes we do.

But that is just the way it is. Women have been making a big fuss over getting married since Fred Flintstone's day.

If you are the mother of the groom, you have one invaluable service to perform in this crucial time in his life. Sit your son down and explain the following to him: Every question his bride-to-be will ask him about the wedding is serious. No matter how trivial he may think it is, every question should be handled with diplomacy and tact. In foreign affairs, the wrong response can cause countries to go to war. What makes him think his wedding is any different?

Tell your son that he has more to think about than renting a tuxedo and choosing a best man. He too has to take responsibility for the wedding. He may not care which photographer to hire, whether to have a band or a disc jockey, or if the centerpieces should be high or low. Tell him that from now on he'd better *learn* to show an interest in the details of the wedding.

And if he can't show a genuine interest, fake one. (It's never too early to learn.)

Let him know that the adorable, kindhearted, gentle girl to whom he proposed is about to become a bundle of nerves. Reassure him that she will return to normal once the wedding is over. Until then, he will have to be more patient and understanding than he's ever been before.

Help your son to understand that his wife-to-be is indeed earnest about making sure this day will be absolutely perfect. That kind of pressure takes a toll on the sweetest dispositions. He will have to go with the flow—or bear the brunt of an uptight, bug-eyed bride.

Don't forget to tell the rest of your family—especially your daughters—that they must be patient and understanding with her. Everybody will have to bite their lips a few times before this wedding is over. Be patient and don't worry. The day after the wedding, she'll be back to normal —or at least away on her honeymoon and out of your sight for a while.

Alas, even though you and your son have done everything to make the planning as painless and easy as possible, this doesn't mean the preparations for the wedding will go smoothly. You may have the Bride of Frankenstein on your hands.

She is the bride who believes that her wedding is *her* day and hers alone, with everything precisely the way she wants it. No one has the right to say no to her.

Be careful. The Bride of Frankenstein is an emotional

bully, picking on everyone around her. In the worst cases, young brides end up bullying not just their husbands-to-be but the groom's whole family as well.

Are there limits to what you must endure? I suppose so, but set the boundaries way out there. If you don't, they'll have to throw a straitjacket on you before the wedding is over.

Years ago, I owned a beauty shop in Queens. On weekends, for extra money, my best friend Jeannette and I made house calls to get brides ready. She did hair, I did makeup.

Too often we found ourselves doing hair and makeup for the Bride of Frankenstein. By the morning of her wedding, that sweet, gracious girl we knew from the beauty shop had become completely possessed.

These mornings always started out the same way: The wound-up bride would announce to all her friends and family in the house that no one could speak to her while she was getting ready, that she simply had too much to do and everyone had to leave her alone. If they disregarded her warning, she wouldn't be responsible for what might happen.

One bride was so wound up that she refused to let her own grandmother into the room while she was dressing. Grandma was left sitting on a bed down the hall. The bride had made her get dressed early so she would be out of the way. The poor woman was all dressed up in her blue gown with a silver bag hanging from her wrist, and her swollen feet in tight shoes dangling from the bed. It was nine o'clock in the morning, and the ceremony was not until four that afternoon. One look at Grandma, and Jeannette and I knew we were in for a rough day.

We tried to relax the bride with some jokes and a few funny stories while we went about our work. She wasn't laughing, and pretty soon neither were we.

The bride's mother came in to tell her that the groom's mother was on the phone and needed to ask a quick question. "Tell her I am all questioned out," the bride announced.

Yes, all brides are nervous, but some brides go too far. They lose sight of others and begin to see themselves as the center of a great spectacle, like Scarlett O'Hara at the ball.

Is your daughter-in-law-to-be telling you what color gown you would look best in? Has she suggested you lose weight? Is she telling all the bridesmaids how to wear their hair? Is she telling your husband what kind of tux will look good on him? Is your husband constantly telling you to calm down?

Has she implied that since her family is paying for the wedding, you must cut your guest list in half? Are your daughters calling you with horror stories about her? Are you starting to dislike her entire family? Is *your* mother-in-law starting to look good?

If you have a bona fide Bride of Frankenstein on your hands, my best advice is to stay away from her. Far away. Keep all personal contact to the barest minimum and tell your family to do the same.

When your son comes homes lugging all her complaints

about you and your family, listen politely. Acknowledge what he's saying ("I'm sorry, we don't *mean* to upset her"), but don't react. These brides are wound up good and tight, and they're looking for someone to pick on. Don't let it be you.

I know you want to pull her hair out when she says some of the awful things the Bride of Frankenstein is famous for saying. But what is giving her a piece of your mind going to get you? You already know what will happen: She is just going to run to your son. Instead of solving your problem with your soon-to-be-daughter-in-law, you will have a bigger one with your son. It's not worth the aggravation.

All your patience and new gray hairs are worthwhile when you see your son get married. You've waited a long time to share this day with him. No matter what happens, enjoy yourself and don't let anything get in the way.

4

*Surviving Your Daughter's Wedding,
More or Less*

BAD WEATHER, bad food, or a bad hairdo won't ruin as many weddings as the aspirations of a frazzled bride who wants everything to be "perfect." If you and your daughter are satisfied with a *nearly* perfect wedding, it takes a lot of pressure off.

There is only one way to insure a nearly perfect wedding: Let your daughter make all the million and one major decisions, from the guest list down to her wedding gown.

A convenient way to think about the wedding is to divide the chores in two. Your daughter will make sure that everyone who attends her wedding is taken care of, so they have a great time at the reception and leave feeling happy and full. Your job during the planning is to make sure she stays calm and in control and doesn't start any wars.

Try not to spoil her. You don't need to, because with the exception perhaps of newborns, brides are probably God's most pampered creatures. From the time your daughter announces her engagement, she will be spoiled and indulged beyond all reason. It's up to you to keep a hatpin ready to burst her balloon every time she starts to drift out of control.

For starters, sit your daughter down and offer her the best advice any mother can give. Tell her that this may be *her* wedding day, but she has an obligation to share it with a lot of other people. It is not hers alone.

Custom and tradition may dictate that the bride's family hold the wedding reception, but that doesn't mean they own it. Does anyone remember the guy she's marrying and his family? This will be *his* wedding day as much as hers. Ideally, a wedding is an event that makes two families happy about the choices their children have made.

So when his parents want to invite a favorite great aunt, after your daughter has decided not to invite any great aunts, let them. You're going to explain to your daughter that *his* guest list is *his* prerogative. The groom and his family should be able to have their favorite people at the wedding—and they should have them without anyone second-guessing whether they belong there.

If the groom's family wants five extra people, tell your daughter not to make a big deal out of it. If his family's guest list is within reason, why insist on absolute parity? The most generous thing you can do for your new son-in-law is to encourage him to be generous to the people he loves on his wedding day.

The bride who understands that her wedding day is something to be shared with others tends to calm down immediately. The realization that her job is to make this day special for the guests takes her out of the spotlight. Of course, nothing prevents a bride from being nervous. But she is a little more settled once she sees her role as being the hostess of a great social event—rather than Queen Elizabeth presiding at her coronation.

The bride is not the only one with hopes and expectations about how this wedding will take place. The groom's mother, too, has been waiting a long time for her child to get married. Your new son-in-law also has a grandmother or two who are overjoyed they're still around to see the happy event. He has family friends across the street who took him camping every summer when he was little. He has a second cousin in Kansas City whom he hardly knows but who was like a sister to his mother a long time ago.

These strange people are not freeloaders. No one invited them because you're picking up the tab. They're part of the groom's life, and they all want a front-row seat to see him and the young woman he's going to marry. They want to be part of the celebration. If they're strangers now, they won't be for long—not if your daughter intends to share in her husband's life. You will make your future son-in-law a very happy groom if your daughter gets a firm grip on this idea right from the start.

Just about the worst thing that can happen to a young bride is to forget that her husband-to-be's family is as important as her own. I've seen more than one couple go down in flames during the planning stages of the wedding. I normally avoid blaming anyone when a couple breaks up. But I can tell you confidentially that when the wheels come off a planned wedding, most of the time it's because the bride was totally out of control.

"I started looking at her and wondering what I ever saw in her," a former groom recalled as he told me what went wrong with his planned nuptials. "She totally disrespected my family and took it out on me. When my sister asked us if we wanted my four-year-old niece in the bridal party, she nearly took my head off. 'If I wanted your niece, I would have asked her,' she told me. 'Who is she to push her daughter into my bridal party? Tell her this is my wedding and she should mind her own business!' What did she mean *her* wedding? What was I, a rent-a-groom? She didn't even ask me if I wanted my niece in the wedding. Well, that was just the beginning; it got worse. She never put anyone else first and ended up attacking every member of my family. According to her, my mother wasn't being helpful and my sisters were getting in the way. I woke up one morning a month before the wedding and said, 'Forget it.' I'd had enough of her. I lost ten thousand dollars, but it was a small price to pay to regain my dignity. It's been a year now, and I haven't once regretted what I did."

That's an extreme example of what can happen, but it's a true one. Weddings make everyone nervous and put a lot of people under stress. In your role as caretaker for your daughter, it's up to you to keep her from becoming a wild woman.

See that you keep a close eye on yourself, too. Every mother of the bride gets upset about something at some point during the planning for a wedding. When issues come up with the groom's family—seating arrangements, guest lists—is it necessary to dump your complaints on your daughter? You'll usually find it easier if you handle whatever problems arise within the families. At such times, see if it's possible to talk things out with your son-in-law's mother. The two of you can usually resolve minor things quicker if you talk directly to each other rather than through the kids.

What do you do when you love the boy she's marrying, but the rest of his family belong on WANTED posters? How's a mother of the bride supposed to react when his family wants to invite twice as many people as was first agreed on? When they demand to be consulted on the menu? When they don't want to drive to the wedding—they want a limo to pick them up at their hotel? When they've got to have it their way or there'll be hell to pay? What do you do when it turns out that your daughter's new in-laws are unbearable monsters?

All you can do is give in as much as your stomach (and budget) can take. My advice is to send the limo, give them veto power over the menu, and negotiate a fair settlement on the number of people they want to invite. What do you do if the demands can't be resolved, when major differences are threatening to turn into major conflict? You may have to have a heart-to-heart talk with your son-in-law—once again, without getting your daughter involved. This is an extreme measure, but if you have to, do it.

First, make sure to keep everyone else in your family—your daughter, your husband, your other children—as far away from the meeting as possible. This talk isn't a secret, it's just private. You don't need any extra confusion from others. When the coast is clear, put your arm around your son-in-law-to-be and ask him to take a walk around the block. Or maybe just ask him to come into the kitchen for a moment.

Start by explaining to your new son-in-law that you are trying to accommodate his family's wishes for the wedding, but that things have not turned out the way you'd hoped. Say you're coming to him because you trust him to recognize what is important about this special day and what is nonsense. Together, you and he can decide what to do about the major issues that seem to be upsetting his family.

Be gentle and avoid saying his folks are being unreasonable. Stifle the urge to tell him you want to strangle every member of his family, one by one. Just say it's impossible for you to do all the things they're asking and you'd like to know —from him—what he thinks are the important ones. Let him know there are choices to be made. Should everyone in his family be put up at hotels or should you cut out the band? You can't afford both. Make it clear you are not asking him to go back to his family and say anything. You just want him to understand what is possible and what is not.

He needs to hear directly from you about the problems, so there are no mistakes or garbled messages. He needs to know what's going on, and so do you. You may convince him to see things your way. He may talk you into some things you hadn't planned on. At least you will be heard.

No two families are ever perfectly the same. Size, traditions, and chemistry vary from one family to another. Maybe your son-in-law has a bigger family than you do. Are you worried that his side of the family will overwhelm yours at the reception? Maybe the expense of extra guests is a real issue and his family offers to pay; however, you wanted to give your daughter's wedding yourself, and you are seriously thinking about turning down the offer.

Apparently it has not yet occurred to you why his family can't cut down their list. What are they going to do, kill off the cousins? Decide who can come by picking names out of a hat?

If all goes right, this will be the one and only time your daughter gets married. Try to give everyone involved what they want, and you will have done your part toward seeing that your daughter doesn't have a second chance at trying to make a perfect wedding.

5

The First Supper

YOUR MARRIED CHILDREN will never let you know it, but your approval means the world to them. Nothing is more valuable. Sure, now that they're married, they are struggling to separate themselves from you. In the process of setting up independent lives of their own, your married children may give you the impression that they couldn't care less what you think. Don't believe it for a minute. They want you to be proud of what they have done on their own.

For most parents, the rite of passage will come when they invite you to dinner at their house for the first time.

Before you ring their doorbell, be aware of some facts.

1. If you are going to take part in the daily lives of your married children, it's important that you never forget that you are a mother—not a friend, not a sister. People can accept (or ignore) just about any dumb remark or unintended slight from their friends, but not from their mothers.

2. You are the most important guest they will ever have. To them, this is an occasion as formal as a state dinner at the

White House, so treat it that way. Can you remember when you were first married and your parents came over for dinner for the very first time? (Worse, remember when your *husband's* parents paid their first visit?) You hoped both families would be proud of you. You wanted them to be pleasantly surprised at what a good hostess you'd become and quietly satisfied that you had chosen the right husband. Now it is your turn to be the person whose opinion everyone is nervous about.

3. As parents, we are prone to take credit when our children excel at just about anything—tap dancing, baseball, the banking business. Whether we admit it or not, we say to ourselves, "See, he listened to me. That's why he's a branch manager already." But the first visit to your married children's house is not the time to say, "I taught her how to make that dish," or "If I hadn't pushed him, he'd still be delivering newspapers." Deep down, these are actually some of the ways of saying how proud we are of our kids and what they've accomplished, but now is not the moment to be indirect about your pride. This is the moment to lavish *them* with credit, gobs of it.

4. The greatest respect we can show for people is the respect we show in their homes. So when you go to visit your married children, there will be no better time than this to give them your approval. If you happen to be looking for proof of how much they care for and respect you, look no further. Just take note of how much work they put into this special night.

Why should you go through all the tiptoeing, please-and-thank-yous, and diplomatic compliments? Because you are entering brand-new territory here. No matter how close you have been to your children, this is new and uncharted land for all of you. Walk with care because you never know what you may step in, if you get my meaning.

Look at it this way: You taught your children how you wanted to run your house. I'm talking about all the things, little and big, that gave you lines around your eyes as a young mother: what time dinner was on the table, how much mess you could tolerate in the den or in their rooms.

Now, in the first days of their marriage, your married children are setting up their own place, probably the biggest thing they have done together so far. Realize that you are in *their* house now and it's *their* turn to make the rules and set the tone. You're dealing with a clean slate.

The first impression you make on them will last a very long time. The most important message to leave behind after your first visit is that you are proud of your married kids and what they have done.

If you're off to see your son's house for the first time, he's going to want you to recognize everything his wife has done. He wants to confirm from the expression on your face that you are quietly proud of him for choosing such an excellent woman. He'll want to know that you're proud he could afford such a great apartment. On your first dinner at your married children's house, even if you find yourself sitting in a fifth-floor walk-up eating off TV trays, be every bit as proud as you'd be if they were living on Park Avenue. He will expect you to compliment them on everything—the curtains in the bedroom, the meal on the table, the shine on the kitchen floor. Nothing will be too small to draw attention.

Look and listen for all your cues. If your daughter-in-law wants to serve you—and you would much prefer to serve yourself—sit down and let her do the serving. Tell them how wonderful it is to be treated like Queen for a Day. Don't get up for anything short of a medical emergency. (On second thought, maybe you should just keel over politely.)

If your daughter-in-law is overwhelmed by too much company and needs help, lend a hand. But don't make a production out of it. A white lie now and then can be a huge kindness. Tell her you're tired of sitting and want to move around a bit. Or just say you want to be with her in the kitchen.

The same rules apply if you're visiting your married daughter for the first time. Remember that she too wants you to be proud of everything that she and her husband have accomplished.

The old familiarities can still be observed at *your* house. Your married kids can still rummage through your kitchen cabinets looking for something to eat. But for the time being, you don't have the same privilege. For now, if you want something, it's better to ask.

Don't let your husband plop into your son-in-law's favorite chair in the living room unless it's offered. Don't let him monopolize the TV remote control. Don't get clannish with your daughter all night and ignore your son-in-law. Talk to him about something other than your daughter. But at some point during the evening, make sure you let him know how happy you are that your daughter chose him.

Show your married children quiet, unmistakable respect in their home, and they will never forget it.

6

House Rules

DO YOUR MARRIED children still swoop into your house without warning? No phone call, no invitation, just the startling sound of the front door swinging open and a voice yelling, "Mom, are you home?"

Did you have other plans for the day? Do your kids care? I didn't think so.

Just because their children act like that, a lot of mothers-in-law feel that they can pop up at their married children's houses in the same way. The mother-in-law who happens to be in the neighborhood and decides to drop by may not be a nuisance to her own child, but to your in-law child, those harmless visits are seen as intrusive. Nothing feels more like an invasion by a police SWAT team than when a mother-in-law arrives unannounced.

If you think that's a double standard, you're right. How come your privacy doesn't stretch much beyond a closed bathroom door, while on the other hand your married children believe their own privacy is some kind of religious relic? It's not fair, but remember, you're a mother-in-law and double standards go with the territory.

Yes, your children lived with you for all those years. Even after they moved out, they still left piles of their junk behind. They probably still have a key to your house. But the person who married your child is not part of that shared history. They're two different people. If it bothers you that your married children walk into your house whenever they please — no call, no warning — tell them that. But just because you let them do it doesn't give you permission to do the same thing.

Married children are entitled to more than just their privacy. Just because they have company doesn't necessarily mean one more guest — meaning you — won't hurt. This may sound unfair and maybe it is, but that's the way they feel.

"My mother-in-law drags her friends and relatives over to my house for visits all the time," said a friend. "No matter what we do, nothing seems to stop her." What's wrong with that? I thought. My son John used to drag his friends to my house for dinner all the time.

But what she said made me think twice: Is it fair for me to do the same thing to my daughter-in-law, now that John is married?

There is going to be a lot of competition for your married children's attention. They work all week, and weekends are their only free time. Just because they live nearby, don't expect them to visit every Saturday or Sunday. Let them come to see you when they feel the urge to be with you. That way no one is under the cloud of obligation. The best times you're ever going to have with your married children are when they are with you because they *want* to be with you.

Don't be afraid that if you don't demand to visit with them you'll never see them. Just say it's been a long time since you've been together and leave it at that. Allow them to do the inviting. You can negotiate a mutually agreeable time and place from there. Let them set the place (your house or theirs) and duration (breakfast, dinner, a couple of days). That's the way you arrange visits with your adult friends, and your adult children should get the same consideration.

7

Equal Treatment

THE MOTHER-IN-LAW with both a married son and a married daughter can be a bundle of contradictions. She looks at her daughter's husband and sees a man who treats her daughter like a queen. She wears the best clothes and drives the latest car. He insists they have a maid. He is so kind and generous to his wife that he belongs in some sort of husband's hall of fame. What a blessing to have a son-in-law like him.

The same woman looks at her son and sees a man who is always under the gun to provide for his grasping wife. He's constantly shelling out money he doesn't have for clothes and vacations. The mother-in-law has never seen her daughter-in-law in the same outfit twice. In between, he is driving her wherever she wants to go. She insists on having a nanny (a stranger!) to help her with her kids. She doesn't lift a finger to help care for her home. Her son is being driven to the poorhouse by his wife's spending. What a demanding wife her son is saddled with!

What's wrong with this picture? Here are two husbands doing exactly the same things, trying to please the wives they obviously love very much. But this mother-in-law sees her son-in-law as a hero and a saint — and her own son as a tragic victim. They can't understand why it isn't clear that their daughters deserve kid-glove treatment while their sons are being taken advantage of. The same picture, two points of view.

The double-standard mother-in-law doesn't realize how unfair she's being. In fact, she has really projected her own wants and expectations onto these two couples. Her son is not allowed to love his wife in the same way her son-in-law loves her daughter. The mother-in-law who can't see that what is good for the goose is good for the gander is missing out on a beautiful relationship — her son's.

8

Money Doesn't Talk, It Screams

*I*F MONEY SCREAMS, just what is it hollering about? Actually, it addresses something vulnerable and sensitive in all of us: the desire for power, the need to be loved, the compulsion to control, and the comfort of security. Power, security, control, love—money means something different to each of us. Maybe it's time you found out what the almighty dollar means to you.

Are your married children about to buy something major you don't approve of: a trip, a house, matching jet skis? Did this influence your decision not to give them the money you had planned? Do you ever hear yourself grumbling that your married children take money from you but don't listen to you? Do they pay more attention to their friends and spend more time with their in-laws than you? If that's true, then *Money is power to you.* You're trying to teach them a lesson with money, show them who's boss by withholding a gift you wanted to give.

Are you giving your married children money you don't really have? It's happening more all the time—parents taking out second mortgages to give their children the down payment on a house of their own or borrowing to give them a car. If this is true, *money to you is a misguided way of showing love.* You feel obligated to come up with the cash to prove that you love them — just like you did when they needed braces or college tuition. A mother will make any financial sacrifice necessary to insure that her children have what they need to grow up. But your son or daughter is married now. Don't feel guilty or pressured to keep paying your kid's way through life. Show love with your concern and support — not with cash you don't have.

When you lavish your married children with gifts you can't afford, you are setting yourself and the kids up for a fall. After you've gone out on a limb for them, it's only natural that you begin to expect things in return. When your children can't live up to those expectations, you feel unappreciated, unloved, even used. That's how resentment creeps into an otherwise easygoing relationship. So skip the loan you can't afford.

Did you ever hear yourself say, "The kids are going somewhere else for Thanksgiving dinner. But when they need money, they sure know where to come." If that thought has a familiar ring, then *money is a means of control to you.* After your married children ask you for money, you seem to think you're entitled to special consideration. If you hadn't given them money, it would be okay for your married child to ignore you on the holiday. Isn't that what you're saying?

Do you give your married children money and then say to yourself, "That felt great. I feel as if I'm taking care of my children and I'm still important in their lives"? If that's the case, *money is security to you*. In fact, you are giving money to your married children not for their sake but for yours. Giving them money makes *you* feel better, because your role in their lives has not changed.

Of course, if you are lucky enough to be able to help your married children without financial strain, please, go right ahead. Absolutely nothing should get in your way. Give them all the help you can, as often as you can.

After you decide to give them money, what rights do you have? You have the right to ask them what they intend to do with it. If you don't like their answer, say no with a clear conscience. But it's never fair to ask about their personal finances. You may ask how they plan to pay you back, but that's as far as you can go. They don't have to give you a financial statement every time they want to borrow a few dollars.

The most important idea to remember is that once you have given them money—and this is important—it is no longer yours. It's theirs.

Suppose you just gave your married kids two thousand dollars to catch up on their bills and the next thing you hear, they've invested in a Peruvian llama farm. This doesn't sit right with you. You begin to question your decision to give them the money in the first place. Know what? It might have been wrong to help them out. But once the money leaves your hands, it's not yours to worry about anymore. If you think your married children can't handle the responsibility of money, don't give it to them. Next time they ask, just say you're sorry but you're a little short this month.

More often than not, the money doesn't matter to you at all. As a mother, I understand that you've spent your whole life monitoring everything your children do. When they started school, you knew every teacher and every homework assignment they ever had — or at least you tried to. You always knew your kids' friends and even tried to know their families. You checked your son's pockets every now and then to make sure he was not getting into any trouble. You helped your daughter pick out her college and probably her first car. I'll bet you paid for both.

So how the heck are you supposed to turn that instinct off overnight? Especially if it involves *your* money? If it upsets you to see them eating out all the time and buying expensive things you don't think they really need, no matter how much your stomach flips, no matter how wasteful you think they are, you're going to have to let them learn on their own. That's life. It's more important to let them make mistakes than to second-guess what you give to them. Give with a clear understanding that your financial help is either a loan or a gift with no strings attached.

Learn to be graceful when giving money. A money gift should be presented openly to *both* your married children. You are taking a big risk by secretly slipping money to your son or daughter. If your married child is sneaking around with money he or she can't account for, you could just be making a bad situation worse. Financial help should be for the benefit of both of them.

Test whether the money is truly for both of them by asking, How does my in-law child feel about this money? Am I giving it as a gift—or because *I* think they need it? Am I telling my daughter, "Look, I know you and your husband are just getting started. Why don't you let me get some new clothes for you?" Sounds generous, right?

This isn't the way your son-in-law may hear it. All this gesture does is tell your son-in-law he is not a terribly good provider. This is not going to make him feel good about himself or about the person who pointed it out to his wife —namely, you.

Try putting a check in an envelope and saying, "I got an extra dividend payment this month and I don't need it." Now that's a gift for both of them.

If you have real concern that your married son or daughter is struggling unnecessarily—is there a gambling problem or drug problem?—sneaking cash is just a temporary solution. It's better to deal with a problem like that in a more straightforward fashion. You're not helping anyone by propping your child up financially.

What about when the shoe is on the other foot? Suppose your married children become successful in their careers and have all the money they could want. Do you find a certain resentment building in you? Do you find yourself thinking,

After all I did for them, it's time they did something nice for me?

Sure, it would be nice if they helped you out or sent you on a vacation this winter, but don't expect it. Feelings like this can end up spoiling your relationship with your married kids. So take a couple of deep breaths and let it go. You put your heart and soul into giving your children what they needed to grow up. You didn't do it to get paid back.

9

A Field Guide to Your In-law Children

BIRD-WATCHERS have those nifty little reference books that tell them everything about the birds they've spotted: markings, mating habits, how they live, all the important details that let bird-watchers know what the heck they're looking at through their binoculars.

With the bird-watchers' books in mind, here is a sort of field guide for mothers-in-law. It is a series of quick thumbnail sketches of some varieties of in-law children who can be particularly hard to handle. It's intended to give you an idea of how they behave and some suggestions for how to act around them.

The Material Girl (or Guy)

HOW TO RECOGNIZE THEM. She (sometimes he) is obsessed with the cost of things. In the eyes of a Material Girl, money is no object; it's a bosom buddy, a soul mate, a living, breathing companion. It sits on her shoulder, whispering in her ear. "That cheap thing? That's not good enough for you! You're worth more than that. Face it, you won't be happy with anything but the best."

The instant you give her a gift, you'll know whether it has reached her (sometimes his) top-dollar standards. Look for the face that's a yard long, the forced smile, the teeny-tiny "thank-you" that slips through thin pursed lips. If you throw a party with a six-foot hero sandwich as the main course, don't expect to hear "nice party, Mom" from her. She may even tell you she's eaten already. If you travel with her, don't figure on staying anyplace with knotty pine paneling.

She wants to dine out first class at every meal. She looks for orchestra seats (on the aisle) for every show she goes to. In extreme cases, she may even start telling your other children how they need a new house or a better car.

HOW THEY ACT. Her dinner parties, her job, her therapist, her computer, her car—whatever it is—will always be the best. If you don't know the cost of these things, don't worry. She'll make sure you are kept fully informed. When she goes out, it's always to the best restaurants, top hotels, exotic vacation spots, snobby beauty salons; what she wears, drinks, eats, and smells like are the best you can buy.

HOW TO HANDLE THEM. First, understand that this kind of snobbery usually masks low self-esteem. Buying and receiving and owning makes the Material Girl (or Guy) feel good.

What's this got to do with you? Nothing. You have to realize her obsession is not a personal attack or a calculated insult to your family. She thinks that if you give her something less than top of the line, you don't think much of her. Worse, she'll think you have no idea who she really is, that you haven't been paying attention. "How can my mother-in-law think I would walk around with a handbag like that —and in that color?"

A suggestion: She likes top quality, so that's what you'll have to give her. At least, the best you can afford. For a $50 birthday gift, you're not going to be able to get a Coach handbag or a Donna Karan evening gown. So get her a Coach coin purse or a Karan T-shirt instead. By saying, "I wish I could have bought you the coat this scarf was on," you're letting her know you understand her. At least she will see that you're trying to give her something she "always wanted." Whatever she does with your gift after that—wear it, exchange it, or give it to the Salvation Army—is up to her.

The trouble only starts when you begin to ask those questions that don't have comforting answers. "Who the hell does she thinks she is, Lady Di?" or "What's the matter, she's too good for cold cuts?" Now *you're* the one insisting that everyone around you live according to your standards.

When she makes condescending comments about your sister's furniture, tell her, "Not everyone has your excellent taste, sweetheart." When she tries to tell you or your children what they should do to move up a notch on the "having" scale, tell her, "You always try to be so helpful. That's what's wonderful about you. But you know, people have to live the way they feel most comfortable." You won't be able to change her high-priced ways. However, you can keep yourself from going broke trying to please her or feeling like a bag lady every time she's around.

Poor Me

HOW TO RECOGNIZE THEM. You always feel so *bad* for them. Your son-in-law or daughter-in-law always seems to get a raw deal from life. He should have had that great promotion, but the boss's nephew got it instead. She can't afford to go to Florida because the kids need braces. The new car they got is a lemon and the dealer won't do anything about it. Why does your in-law child make you feel like you're in the middle of *Days of Our Lives*, without the sexy parts?

Time to wise up and realize that Poor Me in-laws are always sad about something. If they weren't miserable, they wouldn't be happy.

HOW THEY ACT. Poor Me discovered early in life that being upset and depressed all the time is a surefire way to get attention. Everyone has a newer car, a more attentive spouse, better-behaved kids. Everybody else does more favors for members of their family than Poor Me's family does for her or him. Of course, no one is ever required to do as much for the family as Poor Me.

Naturally, you want to make your Poor Me in-law feel better. So you try sending the couple to the movies or a show and arrange for them to have a nice dinner afterward, while you babysit the kids. You're going to show Poor Me a good time or die trying.

So why is it that, the next day, the movie turns out to have been lousy or the seats too close to the stage? Was it inevitable that the restaurant was too crowded or too noisy or the service was slow? Couldn't you have guessed that Poor Me was up for a great night out — but your child was in a bad mood and ruined everything?

HOW TO HANDLE THEM. Do nothing. Nothing you ever try will work for more than a few minutes with Poor Me. It may sound crazy, but it scares Poor Me's to be happy for any length of time. They thrive on the attention the Poor-Me act gets. Trying to make them happy actually ruins their day.

You can spend the whole day trying to make it possible for them to go out. But when the time comes to leave, Poor Me will find an excuse not to go. He or she isn't feeling well. The car is acting up. The newspaper is predicting flash floods.

How do you keep up with Poor Me's? You can't. Don't do anything to make them feel special, and they'll be the happiest people in the world. All they really want is to have someone listen to them complain. He or she is searching for a comrade who will nod sadly and agree that Poor Me was born under a bad sign and, no matter what, nothing ever goes right.

So if you want to be a good mother-in-law (and I know you do), all you have to do is be a good listener. Learn to make a lot of concerned faces. Keep saying you understand what Poor Me is going through, and this in-law child will love you to death.

The Troublemaker

HOW TO RECOGNIZE THEM. At your next family affair, just keep an eye out. Before a Troublemaker daughter-in-law puts her purse down, she will have something negative to say. "How come we were the last to be invited?" Keep watching. Now she's talking to your daughter. "You haven't called us in months," she says. "How come we don't hear from you anymore? We heard you took a trip to New Orleans. Did you have a great time? We really would've loved to have gone too, you know?"

HOW THEY ACT. The Troublemaker in-law child is hard to miss. He or she is compulsively complaining about all the things other people have *not* done for them lately. He is the one who is always ticked off at no less than five people at the same time. Arguing is like a hobby to him. Criticizing and contradicting are how he relaxes. The very idea of a peaceful and happy family event makes him want to run screaming into the night.

And, no matter how much she is poking and pulling at everyone else in the family, she is exquisitely sensitive to how everyone is treating her. "How come everyone got coffee before us? Why are we always the last?" If she isn't getting enough attention or stirring up enough trouble today, she'll bring up ancient hurts, stuff that happened so long ago you had forgotten it. The seating arrangement at Cousin Bob's wedding when they put her practically in the kitchen. The time you forgot to bring the beer and her husband had to make a special trip. No insult or oversight is too old for a thorough rehashing by the Troublemaker.

A mosquito couldn't pass the Troublemaker's nose without some provocative word. Why didn't your niece kiss him hello when she came in? Here's how you should have made the salad. How come no one called his three-year-old daughter on her birthday? If everybody doesn't come over to their apartment for the next big holiday dinner, he's never going to speak to anyone in the family again.

HOW TO HANDLE THEM. Getting along with a Troublemaker is a tough job. They actually have to be reconditioned, so they can hear themselves. Troublemakers can only function if someone is responding to them. If no one is listening (and making excuses for themselves), what is a Troublemaker going to do? They are out of commission.

Don't respond, and let the others in your family fight their own battles. When he asks you why your niece didn't kiss him hello, try this old reliable: "She didn't? Gee, why don't you ask her? She is standing right over there." Maybe the Troublemaker will figure out that you have stopped nibbling at the bait.

If everyone wants to go to the Troublemaker's apartment for the next big holiday, let them. Don't try to stop her when she threatens to call your daughter to complain about not being invited on the trip to New Orleans. Chances are she'll never make that call anyway—not unless you say something stupid like "You wouldn't dare."

Do you really have to answer why she is the last to get coffee or why no one called his three-year-old? It doesn't take a rocket scientist to figure it out. So stop paying attention to the Troublemaker's nonsense.

The Jealous One

HOW TO RECOGNIZE THEM. This in-law child has one question in mind: Why does someone else have something, and I don't? Does someone else *really* deserve that pay raise or that boat or that recognition? The Jealous One doesn't think so.

In fact, the Jealous One has been known from time to time to fly into sudden rages at the unfairness of it all. She worked harder at the gym, so why does someone else have a nicer figure? He thought of that idea first, so why did someone else get credit?

HOW THEY ACT. The Jealous One lives by the motto "Everyone else is better off than I am." He or she is prone to think your family has more than they do and can say such things as "I wish your son treated me like your husband treats you" or "Boy, your daughter is lucky. Her husband gives her everything she wants." Sound familiar?

The other side of jealousy is hating everything others have. "Oh, I would never want a house with that much property." Or "It's a shame the way your brother-in-law takes advantage of his wife's good nature." It's all the same thing—envy. And it's hard to take.

HOW TO HANDLE THEM. If it's any consolation, the in-law Jealous One is not only your problem. Deep-dyed Jealous Ones are jealous of their own mothers too.

They believe they should be treated as special people. They get upset when no one realizes this—or whenever someone else gets special handling. Don't take it personally; you just have to learn to turn them off.

Once you realize Jealous One is not really picking on the people you love—it's just that boundless jealousy talking—you will pay less attention. As you begin to pay less attention, your own anger will recede as well.

There's no way I know of to change Jealous Ones at the core. You just have to see how ridiculous they sound after a while. Didn't you hear him say the other day that it was silly for his sister to go back to law school at her age? Didn't you want to burst out laughing when you heard her complain what a waste it was for her mother to buy such an expensive coat when she hardly leaves the house anymore? Awful, wasn't it?

Just don't pay attention to your Jealous One when he or she gets in that green-envious mood. It's not serious, and you shouldn't be either.

The Competitive In-Law

HOW TO RECOGNIZE THEM. If your daughter gets a new armchair for her living room, all of a sudden the Competitive In-Law has to redo the whole house. Did you accidentally meet a famous person last night while waiting to get your car at the parking garage? Well, the Competitive In-Law has a story about meeting someone even more famous. Did you win a color TV at the church raffle? Your in-law child won a four-day vacation in Cancun once. You mention you're thinking about changing your hairstyle, and the next thing you know, your competitive daughter-in-law is showing off her $200 hairdo from Paul's Palace of Perms.

HOW THEY ACT. Whatever happens to you—whatever you buy, eat, wear, or talk about—the Competitive In-Law has done the same thing too, but better. You're not allowed to be luckier or smarter or more accomplished; it simply won't do. The Competitive In-Law cooks better, dresses better, and dances better than anyone in your entire family.

After a while, it gets ridiculous. You're losing your hair? Hah! They've lost more hair than you had to start with. Fat? They put on (or took off) more pounds than Elizabeth Taylor. The Competitive In-Law can match you tragedy for tragedy: His uncle had more heart attacks; her grandfather was poorer than your grandfather; his family started from nothing before your family started from nothing.

HOW TO HANDLE THEM. Simple, let yourself be topped every time. You can go toe-to-toe or you can give in. When you hear the contest start to heat up, just make a fuss over her Paul's Palace haircut ("That certainly is the *best* haircut I've ever seen") and it mercifully ends right there. What harm is she doing anyway—except maybe to herself? How exhausting it must be to spend all day every day trying to make sure no one outshines you. She's probably been jealous like this her whole life. You have to feel sorry for her, because under that haircut there's really not much going on.

10

Why Do You Want to Know?

WHEN MY SON John first got married, I must have asked him every intrusive question you could think of at least a hundred times. Questions like, Where'd you get that? Where are you going? What are you going to do? Every time, he answered me the same way: "Why do you want to know?" The only answer I could come up with was that I was his mother. Why shouldn't I want to know?

I forgot there is no longer a need to be worried or concerned about my son in the same way I was when he was little. These were all old questions that belonged to another time, now past. He's an adult now, and I wasn't treating him like one. I had to break an old habit, but it wasn't easy.

Is this what life with your married children has come to?

DAUGHTER-IN-LAW *(on the telephone):* Mom, we're going to look for a new car this afternoon, and we'll be right near you. We thought we'd stop by for coffee. Are you busy?

MOTHER-IN-LAW: Oh, I didn't know you were

looking for a car. What's wrong with the old car? I hear all the new ones are very expensive. Hey, my son isn't selling those bonds Grandpa left him, is he?

DAUGHTER-IN-LAW *(deep sigh):* No, Mom.

MOTHER-IN-LAW *(aware that she's in some sort of trouble):* That's a relief. *(pause)* Well, how about if I make you dinner? You know, I don't see you two anymore."

DAUGHTER-IN-LAW: We're going out tonight with friends. Maybe we can come for dinner next week.

MOTHER-IN-LAW *(disappointed):* Who are you going out with?

DAUGHTER-IN-LAW: I don't think you know them. A friend from work and her husband.

MOTHER-IN-LAW: That's nice. So, what time will you be here? I have to know what time to put the coffee on.

What time to put the coffee on? Who is she kidding? She's torturing these poor kids without meaning to. Were any of the other questions really necessary?

It may not occur to this mother-in-law that she's intruding. As far as she's concerned, these are the same questions she has always asked. What's changed?

What has changed is that she is now asking all these highly personal, intrusive questions of someone who already has a mother. What she may have forgotten is that her son (or her daughter) is attached to someone else now—someone who has never answered to you before and I'll bet a bundle has no plans to start now.

You can probably still ask all the questions you've been asking for years, and your own son or daughter will probably answer you in the same reluctant way they always have. But your in-law child may be reluctant to take on a second mom right now. (Most people have a hard enough time surviving one.) Do you blame them? A friend told me the first time her mother-in-law asked her how much a new outfit cost, she got excited thinking her mother-in-law was going to pay for it. Imagine the letdown when the offer never came.

When you start asking all those questions, how do you suppose your in-law child perceives this interrogation? Could it be: "Why is my mother-in-law always in my hair? Why does she have to know the price of everything? Is it necessary for her to know everywhere we go? I would never dare ask her such personal questions. Isn't it *our* business when we are going to have a baby?"

Naturally, when children are young, a mother worries. She spends years trying to guide them and be there when they need a hand. She doesn't want them to make mistakes or to screw up. So she stays on top of them, making sure they don't. What you see in the foregoing phone conversation is the perpetuation of ancient habits formed many years ago.

Have you looked at your kids lately? *Are* they still children? Do these questions really make sense anymore? If you ask yourself why you need to pose all the questions you do, I'll bet you won't ask half of them anymore. Of course, our children will always be our concern, but we have to find new ways to show it.

If you follow these guidelines, the next time your married children call, perhaps the conversations will go like this instead:

DAUGHTER-IN-LAW: Mom, we're thinking about getting a new car this afternoon and, since we'll be around the corner from you, we thought we'd stop by for coffee.

MOTHER-IN-LAW: Oh, that's great! Your father-in-law and I always loved looking at new cars. Well, good luck. I'll be home all day, and I would *love* to see you.

End of story.

11

When You Can Butt In

THERE IS ONLY one time you may speak your mind, and then only with the greatest delicacy. That is when your married child is involved in real danger: some type of physical abuse, a wife's problem with drugs, a husband who drinks or gambles excessively.

You must be absolutely certain that a genuine threat exists before crossing the line. But if you think you have to say something, here's how to do it.

1. First talk to your in-law child who has the problem—not your own child. You must avoid the appearance of starting trouble in their marriage. "Gee, does your husband drink that much all the time?" is not the way to start. Take your concerns first to the person who has the problem. To prove you sincerely want to help, make sure your son-in-law or daughter-in-law understands that you are approaching them privately. No one else needs to know.
2. Plan carefully where and when you will have the talk. Take your daughter-in-law out to lunch. Invite your son-in-law over to give you a hand with something, just the

two of you. Don't start in with anyone else listening. Once you have picked the time and place, don't jump the gun. Barking in the middle of an argument "Go get help!" isn't going to convince them that you have their best interests at heart.

3. Start slowly. Use expressions that will not threaten. Try: "Sweetheart, sometimes people get caught up in things, and before they know it they are at a point where they can't get out. If that happens to you, you know that you can come to me for help." Another way to ease into it is to give your in-law child an example of how you got in too deep—a trip to Las Vegas, where you gambled more than you should have, or a lonely time in your life when you caught yourself drinking too often. "I know I wished I had someone around then to turn to. If it'll help, I'm here for you."

4. Offer your help and support. Say it in this way: "If you want to get some help, I'm here to see you get it." Be gentle and, above all, never attack. If you accuse or attack, you will have blown your chance to help.

5. You may butt in just once. After that, you have to drop the subject, or at least let it go for a while. Most people with problems are usually in some form of denial ("Who, me?"). Or if they recognize they have a problem, they are often defensive ("It's nothing I can't handle"). If you are persistent in offering to help people who don't think they need it, you run out of room very quickly. They begin thinking you're either crazy or trying to start trouble.

That's why I advise you to back off if your in-law child isn't immediately receptive. Once people are on the defensive, they stop listening. Wait for another time or speak to a professional about other ways of dealing with the problem. Be patient, and maybe you'll get another chance.

6. If you've come this far and your in-law child is still listening, count your lucky stars. You can now start to get somewhere. There are support groups for just about everything these days. Help find one—and offer to go along. For a person with a problem, getting help is often the hardest thing to do. The most important thing is the way you approach the subject. The person with the problem has to believe from the start that you're on his or her side.

7. Do not try to help in-law children in any other way than steering them to professionals. Don't give them money. Don't lie for them. Don't make excuses. Don't lend your credit cards. Don't pay off their bills.

8. When the conversation between you and your in-law child is over—no matter how it turns out—keep it strictly to yourself. Tell your in-law child that you intend to keep your talk in confidence. Don't go back to your child and discuss what happened. If your in-law child wants to talk about it with your child, by all means encourage it.

9. If none of this works and the problem is really serious, go get help yourself. You'll need it.

12

Third Wheel

"I WOULD HAVE loved to spend the day with my kids," said my disappointed friend. Her daughter and son-in-law had gone out shopping that afternoon, and when they didn't ask her to come along my friend called to let me know how let down she felt. "They could have asked me, don't you think?"

"I guess so," I said. "But don't feel bad. Maybe they wanted to spend the day alone."

"They *weren't* alone," she shot back. "They had my grandson with them. I would *never* want to go with them if they were alone. Why do you think I'm upset?" She was on a roll now. "It's my son-in-law's doing, I know it," she said. "My daughter would never mind me spending the day with them. Why would he do that? After all I do for them—the baby-sitting, all the running around. If it were *his* mother, I'll bet it would be a different story. His mother doesn't do half what I do." My friend went on in this way for several more minutes, hurt and highly insulted.

Mothers-in-law become entangled in their children's marriages for all sorts of reasons. Sometimes it is because they are divorced or widowed and miss having a family of their own. Maybe they feel they still have an active relationship with their children or they are still needed. In some cases, one of the partners in the marriage gives the mother-in-law permission to be involved. When mothers develop unreasonable expectations for the role they play in their married children's lives, they are setting themselves up for trouble.

It hadn't occurred to my friend that her daughter and her husband had gone out with their toddler so they might talk and be together, just as a family. With both parents working these days, family privacy is a precious commodity. Parents pretty much have to talk in front of their young children about things we might never have mentioned before. Times change.

Being with their children doesn't necessarily mean they aren't "alone." Suppose they want to kiss or just hold hands. This isn't a problem in front of a youngster but perhaps not appropriate if their mothers are around.

At least my friend had the good sense to call me and complain, rather than expressing her disappointment to her kids. What a nightmare it must be to have a mother-in-law who involves herself in everything her married children want to do!

Can you imagine needing a new sofa and having a me-too mother-in-law who says, "When you start looking, let me know; I'll go with you." It sounds so innocent, but how can you say no without causing hurt feelings? Unless you call before you go sofa shopping, your mother-in-law will feel insulted.

I know my friend would never feel slighted if I didn't invite her somewhere. But she doesn't react that way when it comes to her married children. Why? Probably because she feels she *belongs* with them. She always seems horribly disappointed if her kids fail to invite her along. Why else would a mother-in-law put her married children on the spot like that? The considerate mother-in-law might say instead, "If you want company or need any help, just call me. I would love to join you."

The third-wheel mother-in-law thinks it makes perfect sense to go along with her married children to look for a new dining room set. What a coincidence! She's looking for a new dining room set too. An independent mother-in-law who wants company when she goes shopping will make it another day and ask her married children if they would like to join *her*.

13

When the Going Gets Tough, Give Up

OR ARGUMENT'S SAKE, let's say you have the daughter-in-law or son-in-law from hell. One is born every few years and — just your luck — this monster swindled your kid into getting married.

No matter how hard you've tried, you cannot get along with your son-in-law or daughter-in-law. You can't stand to be around them anymore. Your in-law child is disrespectful, inconsiderate, mean, condescending, contradictory, and spiteful. The situation is unbearable. It gives you chest pains.

If your son-in-law is looking for trouble with you, sooner or later he'll find it. If your daughter-in-law keeps pushing your buttons long enough, you're going to react. So what do you do before that happens?

There's only one thing to do — surrender. Give in and give up. At all costs, you have to stop making your relationship with your in-law child into a battle of wills, you versus them. Remove yourself from a fight you don't want to win. That's right — you don't want to win this war of words. Why? Because you may win the war and lose your own child in the fight.

You may be as right as rain, but your own child is naturally going to jump to the defense of his or her spouse the minute you open your mouth to protest. It doesn't matter how legitimate your grievances might be. You are not going to be able to make your son or daughter hear your side of the story. The squawks of a scolding mother are all that will be heard. You don't intend to say, "My heavens, but did you screw up when you married that good-for-nothing!" But that's how it'll sound.

Maybe your child *did* screw up. If your in-law child is really that bad, your son or daughter is probably suffering too. You may not realize it, but your child may know he or she has made a mistake and is stuck being married to a person who can't get along with anyone. If you're complaining or constantly fighting with your in-law child, you are only putting your own child in the middle of a no-win situation.

That's the reason you are surrendering—so your child won't have to be constantly on the defensive. Don't force your child to be the referee between you and your monster in-law. If you want your son to see his spouse clearly, *get out of the way*. Complaining and nagging focuses the attention on you. If you want your daughter to realize the person she is married to is obnoxious, clam up.

All right, you're mad. You're going to think to yourself, How could my son love someone like that? or How could my daughter let him talk that way to her family? Remember you are the older and smarter one. Stay loose and give your own child the room to come to some conclusions.

If you want to avoid the fights that will only drive a wedge between you and your child, it's time to throw up your arms and surrender. Until then, you are just going to have to bear the pain in silence. Nod and smile when your in-law child says those hurtful things. But say nothing. Don't react. What your son-in-law or daughter-in-law is saying probably doesn't need a response anyway, so don't give one. Chances are he or she is trying to get your goat in the first place. Don't get caught in the game. This is probably how your impolite, bullying in-law got attention in childhood and it's how he or she intends to get attention from you.

It takes an iron stomach to ignore insults and bad manners. So why do it? For the sake of your son or daughter, that's why. What is more important, keeping the affection of your children or being right? You may never have peace with your daughter-in-law or son-in-law from hell. But if you stop butting heads, at least you have a chance to get your own child back. As long as this unreasonable in-law child is married to your son or daughter, treat her or him with all the caution and care you'd give someone who was holding your child for ransom. You simply can't afford to put your own child on the spot.

How do you surrender? Pretty simple. Ignore your unpleasant in-law child *no matter what*. Like a bad rash, don't scratch it and pray it goes away.

First step: Start to keep visits with your married children to a minimum. If you're used to going to their house for dinner, try making a date for lunch or brunch instead. If that doesn't work, try a meal with an even shorter attention span, like coffee or dessert. Find out what lengths of time you can spend comfortably with them and stick to it.

Make excuses to see your child alone. Try meeting your son or daughter for lunch at work or make shopping dates. This way, you can see your child at least occasionally without offending the offending spouse.

For heaven's sake, don't use these visits with your own child to bash your in-law child. Remember, you're supposed to be ignoring the unpleasantness, not complaining about it.

Once you've made it clear you are not going to react, there are only a few ways your overbearing in-law child can respond. He or she will pay less attention to you—because you aren't reacting. So you can expect fewer visits (thank heavens) after he or she begins to turn elsewhere for the negative attention they crave.

If you're very lucky, sooner or later your dreadful son-in-law will learn that you are a bad playmate for his nasty games and he won't want to play with you anymore. Your awful daughter-in-law may even learn a little respect for you and quit. Don't count on it. But weirder things have happened.

14

Who Asked You?

*T*HE LAW of the jungle is plain: Mothers have a God-given right to know everything their children are doing all the time. It is a kind of divine swap. Mothers take care of their children's every physical and emotional need for fifteen or twenty years and, in exchange, they are allowed to go through their kids' drawers, rifle their pockets, and read their diaries. It is a beautifully balanced thing, the mother-child relationship. Children get to go into your handbag without asking, and you get to search under their mattresses.

This is how it works for the first decade or two of a child's life. It is perfectly appropriate, acceptable behavior — for both of you. Every time your child rebelled against your rules and restrictions you sat and listened, but you rarely budged or gave in. You had a parental obligation to know what your child was up to. You didn't give up imposing a curfew just because they sulked in their rooms or stamped their feet.

It was hard enough for me when my son went to college and I could no longer visit his teachers to find out how he was doing in school and discuss his grades. It was murder when he got married. The trip was short and painful. I went from being a full-fledged, fully functioning, and—let's say it—crackerjack mom to being an annoying, obnoxious, oh-it's-you-again mother-in-law. The transition happens in an instant and, frankly, few mothers are prepared to handle it. One day, this child is yours. The next, he is reacting to the things you say with a pained expression on his face that makes you want to slug him.

If you were a hands-on mother like I was, it was hard giving up this divine arrangement. All those years of knowing what your child was doing, thinking, whom he or she was seeing—all of sudden, they vanish without a trace when your child gets married.

What's more, if this transition is not made with the same precision as the cutting of a diamond, you may regret it for many years. Recognizing the difference between when to say something and when to bite your tongue is practically a survival skill—like knowing which roots and berries you can eat when you get lost in the woods. So here is a lesson in the fine art of knowing when something is none of your business and—on rare occasions—when you may put in your two cents.

After a lifetime of telling your child what to do, you will now have to begin to recognize certain boundaries. The first and most important border is this: *Don't give advice or express an opinion unless you have been asked.*

Why don't we stop and let that sink in.

Before offering your thoughts, your insights, before shar-
ing the years of your superior experience with your married
children, ask yourself, Have I been asked? If you haven't
been asked what you think, how you feel, or what your
opinion is, don't offer it.

It's not easy, I know. For instance, your married children
take you to see a house they're thinking of buying. If you
think they're looking for your opinion, save yourself the trip.
Don't even bother getting into the car.

What they actually want is your approval, plain and simple. You're being shown the house for one reason — they
want you to like it. So like it. Remember you don't have to
live there. In fact, I'll bet your married children probably
know already what you will like and dislike about the house.

Kids are very sensitive to their parents' prejudices. That's
why the first thing they'll show or tell you about is some
characteristic of the house they know you will approve of. If
you're a gardener, they'll talk about how big the backyard is.
If you don't drive, they'll tell you how close the train station
is. If you complained all your life about not having enough
closet space, they'll boast about how many closets there are.
They'll lead off with something they know you'll like —
because they are looking for you to say yes.

I know kids sometime beat around the bush when they
want something, and you may suspect from time to time
that your married children are being subtle or asking indi-
rectly for your opinion. When you can't tell for sure, assume
you are wrong. Respond only to the direct and unmistakable

request: "Mom, what do you think?" That way, there are no misunderstandings.

I know you only want to help your married children. No mother-in-law sets out intending to make a mess of her kids' affairs. You want to make sure they don't screw up or get taken advantage of. Unfortunately, you can't take away their opportunities to make mistakes. They will have to live their own lives.

Some mothers-in-law just cannot help themselves, just cannot shut up. They are the Nosy Rosies of this world. We all know a Nosy Rosie or two. She is the mother who says, "I can ask anything I want; I'm the mother," or "I raised him, he didn't raise me," or "If you're smart, you'll listen to me." Do you recognize her?

Whatever Nosy Rosie does, she does it with all her heart and good intentions. She believes she's just trying to help. When she's through helping, Nosy Rosie doesn't understand why her married children want to murder her.

She doesn't like the fact that her daughter-in-law is at her sister's or her mother's house every night after work and never at home with her son? Her first impulse is to march over to his place and demand to know why he doesn't put a stop to it. Her next urge is to call up her daughter-in-law and tell her to go home right now. The first time her daughter-in-law says something evenly mildly critical about her son, Nosy Rosie goes for the throat. "Look who's talking! Don't tell *my* son what to do. Why, you're nothing but—" Whoa, Rosie. Stop right there.

Seems that Rosie has an uncontrollable urge to offer her opinion, but she needs to mind her own business. What goes on between her son and his wife is his concern.

The next time she thinks her poor son is home all alone, she might suggest to her husband that he go over and watch the ball game with him. Or she might invite her son and one of his friends over to eat. (The friend part is important. She doesn't want to make the invitation seem like an implicit criticism of her daughter-in-law.) The trick is for Rosie to be attentive and loving to her own child—without making him feel that she is judging his marriage or his wife.

Is her son an auto bug? She could ask him to come over to look at something under the hood of her car. The point is to come up with positive ways to occupy her son's time and energy. In that way, she is not upsetting herself that her son is being neglected.

Ultimately, I suspect Nosy Rosie will find out that what bothers her so much does not matter to her son in the least. He may prefer to lie on the couch with the TV clicker or a book. The peace and quiet of an empty house may be exactly what he's looking for. With a new approach, Rosie has half a chance of discovering the truth. She may have misjudged the situation from the start.

Another example: Say Nosy Rosie's daughter is married to a guy who can't seem to find himself and drifts from job to job. He doesn't seem anxious to settle down to anything. Rosie suspects he is becoming a real sponge, living off her daughter's accomplishments and income. Her first urge is to tell her daughter she's made a serious mistake and to get rid of the clown before it's too late.

Why won't that work? Here's one reason. Very successful people often see themselves as being successful at just one thing. Rosie's daughter-the-lawyer feels confident that she can handle a cranky judge, but she doesn't know what to say to the garage-door repairman. She thinks she has to rely on other people — like her husband — to do that for her.

The minute she hears Rosie suggest she get rid of her sponging husband, it sounds unmistakably as if her mother is picking on her — again. Only positive talk will open people's eyes to see they are perhaps not as limited as they might have thought. Rosie will get much further by letting her daughter hear how accomplished she is. "All your hard work and talent have paid off," Rosie might say. "No matter what happens, darling, you can always depend on yourself." That's a positive move.

One more example: Rosie thinks her daughter-in-law is spending way too much on clothes. She's wild, out of control at the mall. Rosie is dying to warn her that she's headed for financial trouble if she keeps it up. At that moment, Rosie needs to ask herself, Who can say to me that I'm spending too much on an outfit? Who has the right to say that to me? *Maybe* my husband. (And I stress *maybe*.) But no one else, not even my best friend. What I spend is simply nobody's business.

So she gives her free-spending daughter-in-law the same respect she expects for herself. Score one for Rosie.

Suppose Rosie's son-in-law plays basketball with his friends every weekend when she feels he should be spending more time helping her daughter with the kids. To Rosie, this sounds at first like a perfectly legitimate gripe.

But Rosie is beginning to understand that it won't help a bit if she tells her daughter that her husband is selfish and spoiled. (Or what Rosie would do if he was *her* husband.) She doesn't want to make her daughter more unhappy than she may already be. Instead, she tries spending more time with her daughter. Or she offers to watch the kids for her on the weekends. Again, Rosie has figured out how to turn her frustration into something positive.

In the end, the things that keeps us up nights worrying about our kids are usually not the same things that are bothering our children. A mother-in-law once told me that she resented her son-in-law whenever he came for a visit with her daughter. He was always on the verge of rushing them home early, and her daughter was never able to relax. Actually, the daughter, who was a client also, wasn't crazy about her husband either. But at times he did come in handy, she told me, like when she wanted to make a quick getaway from her mother's house. She'd poke him secretly, and he would instantly say they had to leave. Worked every time, she said.

15

When They Battle

EVERY TIME you're out in public with your married children, do they fight like two bad kids? Have you heard them speak horribly to each other — really nasty, ugly talk — in front of the rest of your family? At times, have you seen them raise their hands or throw things at each other? It makes you want to crawl under a table and die, doesn't it?

Their anger seems to show no boundaries, and it appears as if they want to drag everyone else into their marital squabbles. Then the next day they are the best of friends again, loving, smooching, not a hair out of place. The battle is over. Every unkind word between them is completely forgotten. And they can't understand why *you're* upset.

You are left asking yourself, What the hell was that? What just happened?

To them, what happened was no big deal because they do it every day. It's just how they are. Some couples can't relate to each other in any other way than with anger. They have to fight in order to establish some kind of rapport with their partners. They act this way in front of you and the rest of the family because their knock-down drag-outs are not real to them. They see no reason to hide them. In fact, they're offended you would dare to mention it to them because they see their battles as perfectly normal.

Do any of these phrases sound familiar? "If we have to go to dinner at your mother's house, we are leaving early" or "If you want to stay, then stay, but I'm leaving" or "It's my mother and you'll show some respect." At full volume, these are the sounds of a battle for supremacy. It's a fight to see who will get to call the shots. As soon as it is established — usually one or the other gives in — they are back to normal, or what passes for normal with them.

Sometimes, simple jealousy will set a couple off :

ONE PARTNER: Every time we're with your family, you ignore me. You don't even know I'm around.

OTHER PARTNER: Is that why you cause a fight every time we're out with my friends or my family?

That's all it takes. They're at each other's throats again.

Where does it say that you and other family members have to put up with this kind of behavior? Absolutely no one — especially a mother-in-law — should have to look the other way when their kids start fighting with each other. If your married children won't show respect for each other in front of you, you do not have to hear their constant bickering. It's that simple.

How can you *not* invite them to family dinner when they

are your family? Easy, just don't. When they ask you why they weren't invited, restrain yourself from what you really want to say ("You two act like a couple of brats and have embarrassed me for the last time"). Instead, try to be gentle but straightforward. "I didn't know how the two of you would be getting along on that day, and I didn't want to share in another of your fights. It hurts me to see the two of you go at each other. I know it's none of my business, I know. According to you, it means nothing; you'll be best friends again in two minutes. But I can't handle it, so I have decided not to invite you to any more dinners. I'm sorry to have to do this, but I can't think of any other way to deal with this situation."

Make sure you are not telling them how to behave themselves. Don't rehash any of their past brawls but simply explain that you don't want to be around that kind of behavior any more. It has just gotten too painful. You simply no longer want to be a part of it, plain and simple. How they treat each other is their business, but you don't want to be ringside.

When you speak to them, do it when they are together. This way they can't put the blame on their spouse — "It's your daughter who always starts with me" or "When he has a couple of beers, he starts picking on me." That's a tar pit for a mother-in-law.

Don't let them put you in the middle. "When he can't have his way, he gets nasty" or "She's always bitching about me." These are your exit cues. Just before you leave, assure them that if they change their behavior, you would love to have them back again.

If they don't make a conscientious effort to stop fighting in front of you, you'll feel bad for a while. But sooner or later, you'll get used to the peace and quiet of being with the rest of your children and their families — without the fear that your two brawlers will start in again.

If all else fails, here's a trump card. Get a doctor's note saying something about how you must avoid stress for health reasons. Cough a little and hold your chest if they start going at each other again. That will remind them that you're a "sick" woman.

16

Loose Lips

THE NERVE of some kids these days! They really think they can say whatever they want, to whomever they want. Can your daughter-in-law really be calling your son a jerk right to your face? Maybe your ears deceived you but you could swear your son-in-law just told you your daughter is a spoiled brat.

Old-fashioned respect has become just that, old-fashioned. Manners aren't what they used to be. Sometimes it seems that common courtesy belongs in a case in the Smithsonian, right across the way from George Washington's wooden teeth.

In your day, you would no sooner tell your mother-in-law that her son was a slob (no matter how tempting or true) than you'd track mud on her just-waxed kitchen floor. It simply wasn't done.

Why is it that your in-law children have an uncontrollable urge to run down your child in your presence? Can't your son-in-law see it hurts your feelings? Does your daughter-in-law think you're made of wood? If she wants to talk that way, why doesn't she do it at home where you don't have to hear it? Is there anything you can do about it?

Yes, there is. But first you might want to consider the possibility that what you're hearing may not be as bad as it sounds. I was lucky, and I found out the easy way.

One night, my daughter-in-law Mary began complaining to me that my son was not a big help around the house. Not only was John sitting right there but so was Mary's mother.

"Mary!" cried her mother. "How can you complain about John like that to his mother?"

"Oh, Mom," said Mary, unconcerned, "John's mother knows how he can be." She turned to me, " Right, Mom?"

Mary saw nothing rude about complaining to me about John. Why? Because, I realized, Mary wasn't talking about my son. She was complaining about her husband. It was the same guy, but two different people.

I'd complained a thousand times about my own husband —when I found him every Saturday morning in the breakfast nook with his nose in the newspaper instead of mowing the grass or taking down the screens as he'd promised.

In fairness, I realized I couldn't be upset with Mary. The only thing she'd done wrong was forget that she was talking to John's mother. She simply assumes I know that she's talking about her husband—not my son. She assumes that I know what she's saying is true, which it usually is.

I wouldn't be offended if a friend told me what a bonehead her husband was for forgetting their anniversary again. It doesn't matter that I knew her husband long before I knew her.

Judge for yourself. When your own daughter talks sharply about her boyfriend in front of you, do you get upset? Of course not. That's because you're listening to her with the ears of a friend and a mother. People complain about the faults and failures of their spouses all the time. It's as American as calling the umpire blind. You can't be offended just because the umpire happens to be your son.

So how do you handle it?

If you really can't get over the uncomfortable feeling, you could casually say to your in-law child, "I don't know why I'm so sensitive when you get upset with my son [or daughter]. I know you never get upset without good reason. I think you're really a very patient person. As a mother, when I hear you talk like that, I think I have to say something in his [or her] defense. I know it's only because it's my child, but that's the way I feel." Your in-law child may come to realize how uncomfortable you are with these comments.

The other alternative is to learn to listen with the ear of a friend, the same way you listen to your sister or neighbor. Just keep saying to yourself that your daughter-in-law isn't talking about *your son*, she's squawking about *her husband*. That's a woman's legal right—it says so right on the marriage license. Or if it doesn't, it ought to.

17

More Loose Lips

A MOUTH IS a dangerous weapon in the wrong hands. It can cause trouble far beyond the person who can't learn to control it.

How many mothers have you heard complain about their sons-in-law, "He doesn't do a thing for my daughter. She works and raises the kids and takes care of the house without any help from him." (The other half of the equation is the mother-in-law who says, "My poor son, his wife is never home.")

I've heard that kind of talk for years. What I always wanted to know was; what gave her the idea that her son-in-law never helps with the kids? How does she know that her daughter-in-law is never home?

The answer is she *doesn't* know these things firsthand unless her own son or daughter tells her. Resentful mothers-in-law get their resentment handed down from their complaining children or some other gossipy family member.

Mothers are very protective creatures. They are easily suckered into the trap of taking their married children's complaints too seriously. Most often, the children are just sounding off—venting a little steam—and it means nothing beyond the moment.

The complaining kids are then amazed to discover that their mothers have grown to dislike their husbands or wives. They can't understand why their even-tempered mothers seem to be cold to their spouses, picking on every little mistake or misunderstanding.

"My mother knows how much I love Dorothy. So why is she so critical of my wife lately?" a son asks. What does this kid expect after grumbling to his mother about how Dorothy maxed out all the credit cards? Or how Dorothy leaves the laundry piled up for weeks? Or how Dorothy's mother practically *lives* with them these days?

The last thing a mother wants to hear her daughter say is that her husband stayed out until 5 A.M. playing cards, he never helps around the house, and he's so cheap he still has money from the tooth fairy. When their mothers suddenly have nothing nice to say, why do these complaining children wonder what happened?

Children are used to going to Mom to complain about their siblings ("he stole my truck!") and their teachers. Their mothers usually calmed them down and sent them on their way. When it was over, Mom didn't hate their little brother or their chemistry teacher. Even after children are grown up, some still expect their everyday complaints to get the same motherly reaction. As children, they simply want you to be mad at their spouses when they are—and then make up with them the next day when they do.

Obviously, that may be a bit too much to ask. Maybe you can't stop your children from running off at the mouth with every little complaint. But realize that your children may not want you to take to heart everything they say.

Some mothers can't seem to forget the bad things they heard their in-law children have done. That's when it is time for their children to stop dumping bad news on their parents and then acting the next day like nothing happened.

If you can't be perfectly objective about the ups and downs of their relationship, maybe you should tell your children that. Tell them that, because you love them, it's hard for you to ignore every hurt and annoyance their marriage produces. So perhaps it's best if they share a little less with you about what's going on at home.

I can imagine some mothers aren't going to like that idea, fearing their children won't tell them anything anymore. Please, you should be so lucky.

They'll still keep coming to you, don't worry about that. But they may begin to think a little before complaining to you quite so much.

18

How to Make Up
After a Really Bad Fight

IT TAKES a big person to walk up and look someone in the face and say, "I was wrong and I'm sorry." It's even tougher when you think you weren't at fault and the person you're apologizing to was, in fact, the cause of all the trouble. Now *that's* genuine heavy lifting. When you're fighting with your in-law children and you want to stop, making up begins only after you put aside the blaming and admit you were wrong.

It doesn't matter how things got this bad. Stop racking your brain trying to figure out what you did that made your own children stop speaking to you. Maybe it started innocently, but you can't think about that now.

How wrong your married children are or how much to blame they are for the bad behavior and bad manners that started the argument must be forgotten. If you want to bury the hatchet and get back together with your in-law children, what matters now is that you take some of the blame too. It's a start.

Ultimately, you don't have to come to the conclusion that you were totally wrong and they were completely right about everything. Just as a stopped clock is right twice a day, your offending son-in-law or daughter-in-law was right about *something* in the mess in which you find yourself. If you want to get back to the way things used to be with your married children, you need to own up to your mistakes. Then you can move on.

To start, you will need to find a mediator, someone who can act as a go-between. Select a person who knows both you and your in-law child pretty well. It's best not to use someone from either immediate family. The idea is to find a friend who can speak for both of you without fear. Your husband or one of your other children may be too close for in-law children to accept; they need to feel the mediator has their best interests at heart too. You're looking for someone who will do more than carry a message for you. Your mediator should be someone whom your in-law child will trust.

Once you have chosen someone, go and tell the mediator you'd like help in making peace again with your in-law child. First things first. Tell the mediator you have made mistakes in the past and no beating around the bush. Admit it right away: "I screwed up." Describe what you did that caused the falling out.

Even if you think your daughter-in-law or son-in-law was the monster who started the whole thing, you're going to have to drop your grievances. Letting go of whatever insult or hurt was inflicted on you is harder than admitting you did something wrong. You have to be willing *not* to discuss with the mediator what your in-law child may have done wrong. Bury it and forget it. Apologize without any excuse. Don't explain it, rationalize it, or tell your side of it. Take responsibility and say that all you want now is to make a new start. That's why you chose a mediator who knows you both. For peace to come, you need someone who can say credibly, "Look, if your mother-in-law came to me and said she was sorry, she has to be sincere."

If there isn't any person like this, try writing it in a letter to your in-law child. Say you are sorry for what happened and you want to put the bad times behind you.

For the first meeting, propose something short, perhaps a cup of coffee. After extending the olive branch, leave the next step to your married children. Let them pick the time, the place, and the cast. Don't try to dictate who should or shouldn't be there when you meet. Leave all that up to your in-law child.

This first meeting may be awkward and uncomfortable, but you won't be able to do anything about that. Your in-law child will probably feel the need to go back over all the old grievances and take a few of more whacks at you. If you anticipate it, you'll be better equipped to handle it without reacting. When the floodgates open, nod sadly and say you're sorry. Try to hold back the urge to express your own displeasure—if you can.

If your in-law child wants you to explain your position on the problems, go ahead and say what's on your mind. "I got mad at you because..." or something like that. But try adding at the end, "I was wrong, and I know that now."

19

When Your Child Is Gay—
or You Are

PERHAPS THINGS didn't turn out exactly as you'd planned. There will be no marriage in the traditional sense, no church wedding, no cake cutting, no video or wedding album to show your friends — and probably no grandchildren. But just because your son or daughter is gay doesn't mean you will not be, in every sense of the word, a mother-in-law. You won't get off that easy.

Look at the bright side. You've already been through the toughest part. A long time ago, you accepted that your son or daughter is gay and not leading the sort of life you expected. If you are one of those mothers who has no problem with the fact that your son or daughter's life partner is of the same sex, I expect you will have most of the same garden-variety problems mothers-in-law all over the world must endure, including in-law children who are unappreciative and think they know it all.

If you have not reconciled yourself emotionally with your child's partner — or if your gay son-in-law or daughter-in-law won't accept that you want to remain a big part of your child's life — well, fasten your seat belts. It's going to be a bumpy ride.

Let's say you and your child have a perfectly open relationship. You've known about his or her sexual orientation for years and it's no big deal. Let's say your gay son-in-law or daughter-in-law has not been so lucky. Their family simply doesn't know who their child is. Or, worse, they *do* know and they blame your kid for it. Naturally, it makes a mother want to fight back against the injustice of it all.

Are you thinking, I'll just invite the other parents to my house to talk it out, and once we all get to know each other a little better, everything will be fine?

Well, that may sound like a good idea, but it's not. As bad as you feel for your gay kids, you're not going to be able to rescue them. Forget about being the hero who helps another mother (and father) come to terms with the facts of gay life you may have accepted long ago. They'll just have to go through it themselves.

Pushing yourself into this delicate matter is only likely to double their trouble. What do you think happens when you phone the other parents and discover that they don't want to meet you or even discuss it? All you've done is put your child's partner on the spot. Leave it to your kids and the other parents to make their own peace.

Meanwhile, don't take it personally. Don't keep suggesting to your kids new ways in which the other parents can come to grips with their relationship the way you did. If you constantly ask your child's partner about how things are going with his or her parents, you force your child and the partner to go over painful, uncomfortable feelings. Soon you'll be identified with those bad feelings. It's true in any relationship. What had only been a problem with his or her parents suddenly becomes a problem with you too. It's very annoying to keep constantly updating you on a lousy predicament. Avoid the pressure that's going to make your son or your daughter's partner feel bad or out of place. They are having a hard enough time as it is.

Staying out of the middle of your gay kids' lives can be a real test of your tolerance. Is the rest of your family uncomfortable about including your child's partner in family occasions? You realize, of course, that you can't tell other people who they can and can't invite to their weddings, bar mitzvahs, christenings, or any of the other rites of family life. So what are you supposed to do about the snubs when you don't control the guest list?

If your gay child's partner isn't invited to a family wedding, don't threaten not to attend either. This only polarizes things. One way to handle it without hurting anyone's feelings is to go to the ceremony and then go home. Skip the reception. You'll have done the right thing, and caused as little confusion as possible. Go to the synagogue for the bar mitzvah, the church for the christening, whatever. Pay your respects in the warmest way you can—and leave.

Is your problem with your gay in-law closer to home? Do *you* have a hard time inviting your child's gay partner to family functions? Ask yourself some obvious questions. Are you afraid that others will realize that your child is gay if your son or daughter shows up for the holidays with a partner of the same sex? If that's what's bothering you, relax. I'll bet they've known it at least as long as you have.

A seventy-year-old grandmother knocked my socks off during a session when she blurted out, "I don't think my daughter understands that my grandson doesn't like girls."

"What makes you say that? I asked.

"My oldest brother never liked girls either. My mother was always trying to get him married, but I knew he never would."

I nearly fell off my chair. This woman's daughter had been sneaking around for years trying to shield her family from the fact that her son was gay, and the grandmother knew all along. What's more, she accepted it before her daughter did. Don't underestimate the rest of your family — they can take care of themselves.

What do you do when your children will not accept a gay in-law? This is a rough one. On an everyday basis, most mothers learn how to handle the friction. Contact between your gay kids and the rest of the family is only occasional anyway, but oh, those occasions!

Holidays have become a regular nightmare for you. You dread them and grow more miserable every year as December approaches because you anticipate another tense, unhappy family gathering. The solution isn't simple, but first let me tell you where the trouble starts.

It begins when you insist the entire family celebrate these things together, no matter what. When you, as the mother, expect everyone to sit at the same table because that's the way you think a family ought to be, it's no wonder it ends in fireworks. You probably feel that because you do everything for your family all year long, they ought to act decently for just one day. You're right. But as bad as you feel about giving up those big family days you have dreamed of, it won't feel as bad as the fights and mangled feelings that result when you put people together who really don't want to be there.

All families have special problems. The smart ones learn how to accommodate themselves to their difficulties. The moment you insist that family members sit down together like an episode of *The Brady Bunch,* your dream becomes their nightmare.

You don't have to exclude your gay child and his or her friend from family functions to keep the peace. Instead, plan on two celebrations for the holidays. You can invite your gay child and his or her partner over at a time when your other children are elsewhere—say, visiting *their* mothers-in-law. Or you can split the holidays between your children. It hurts a mother terribly to do that, but if people can't be together in love and respect, we can't force them to.

When it's your birthday or your husband's, plan *two* parties and have *two* cakes. Do it once for those people in your family who cannot handle your child and his or her partner —and do it again for your gay kids.

The most heartbreaking problem is when your husband will not accept your child's partner. You can't insist that he accept your child's gay life and gay lover. If you try to force him to think as you do, he is likely to dig in his heels and resist even more. Your only alternative is to maintain your relationship with your gay kids outside the home. Go to dinner with them or visit them at their place. It's not fair to put either your child's partner or your husband on the spot.

Finally, what do you do if you, the mother-in-law, are gay and your in-law child has a hang-up about it? Is your companion invited when you are asked to dinner at your married children's house for the holidays? Is your daughter-in-law or son-in-law uncomfortable with you and your partner? It's no news that your sexual orientation makes some people ill at ease. Are you being subtly cut out of your child's life? Is it easier for your son or daughter to exclude you from their family life than it is to deal with his or her spouse? Getting around problems like these isn't simple.

Again, family hassles usually begin when you demand your rights as a mother. What mother doesn't want to have her family together for the holidays? What loving, sensitive person (gay or straight) can go out for the evening to a party or a wedding and leave her partner at home with a chicken potpie and the *TV Guide*? Your natural instinct is to put your foot down and insist that your children and their spouses accept you and your companion exactly as you are. You accepted them, after all. If that's how you're going to act, then expect the conflict you have invited.

At least in the beginning of your child's marriage, you'll have to find out what is possible. Can your in-law child deal with Mother's Day dinner at the house you share with your partner? Before you insist on inviting your son-in-law to your birthday party, ask yourself, Does he really have to be there? Not everybody has to be dragged to every family affair. Let your reluctant in-law child off the hook by saying you'll understand if he doesn't want to come. The idea is to come up with some arrangement that will free up your own child to come without putting the spouse on the spot. (I'm convinced that letting people off the hook is actually a type of love — and an underrated one too.) The more understanding you show your in-law kids, the easier it will eventually be for them to come into your world and accept your choices.

In the meantime, keep a hold on your temper. As the mother-in-law, you are supposed to be the older, more mature person in this parent-child relationship. No matter how much your feelings are hurt, you'll have to give your in-law child some time to accept what's going on.

Until then, stay in touch with your own child by phone. See her or him as much as you can outside the house. Go out to dinner, lunch, and the movies or take short vacations together, just the two of you. Create as little confusion as possible in the lives of your married children. If there are not too many casualties and you can keep your relationship as smooth as possible, your son-in-law or daughter-in-law will come around in time.

20

Answers to the Questions You're Dying to Ask

*I*F YOU COULD ask your son-in-law or daughter-in-law any question you wanted without worrying that you'd be thought of as nosy or intruding, what would it be? Here is a list of some of the burning questions that mothers-in-law are usually afraid to ask. And here's what their in-law children might say, if they weren't afraid to answer.

Q: *Why doesn't my in-law child want to be with our family for the holidays?*

My mother-in-law tries very hard to be the glue of her family, and that's what makes holiday time at her house so stressful. She gets excited and hopes, when everyone comes home for the holidays, that everything will be back to normal. It should be fun and relaxing, but my mother-in-law's holidays aren't like that. She puts too much emphasis on the whole family being together, when the truth is her family just doesn't get along that well. She makes a big fuss because she feels, if she can pull off one big day, it will make up for all the problems her family has the rest of the year.

My mother in-law doesn't know that my wife is the one who doesn't want to go to her mother's house anymore for the holidays. She can't take the stress. By the time the ball drops in Times Square on New Year's Eve, my wife realizes it's a brand-new year—but she's got the same old family. She prefers being with my family on holidays because there are no expectations and no disappointments.

If it makes my mother-in-law feel better to blame me, so be it. But my in-laws had their problems long before I came along.

Q: *Why doesn't my in-law child call me "Mom"?*

This is hard to talk about, but I have a hang-up about calling my mother-in-law "Mom." It's got nothing to do with her. It's just that I already have a mother, and I'd feel uncomfortable calling someone else by that name. I know everyone does it, but when I try to call my mother-in-law "Mom," it somehow doesn't sound natural. I'm sorry, but that's the way I feel.

It causes some real problems too. How do you get someone's attention when you can't use her name? I'd be uncomfortable calling my mother-in-law by her first name, and calling her Mrs. B sounds too formal. So I have to wait for her to turn around and look my way before I can start a conversation. Frankly, I try not to talk to her unless she says something to me first. It's awful.

I can't say anything about this to her because I'd feel awkward. I wish she'd just say to me, "I don't know why I never told you this before, but it's perfectly all right if you want to call me Kaye." I'd be *so* relieved.

Q: *When I buy my daughter-in-law a gift, why do I never see her wear it?*

It's nothing to start a family war over, but this is getting out of hand. Both our feelings are getting hurt. I say to myself, "My mother-in-law just doesn't have a clue about who I am. If she did, she would never have bought me something like *this* to wear." And she must be saying to herself, "My daughter-in-law doesn't like me because she hates everything I buy for her."

You know what the problem is? My mother-in-law and I just don't have the same taste. I appreciate that my mother-in-law likes to buy me gifts. I don't understand why she keeps buying me clothes. Does it look to her like I *need* clothes?

I wish she would make life easier on herself and give me a gift certificate instead. I'd be happy to show her what I bought.

Q: *Why is it when someone comes to visit unexpectedly at my married child's house, it's called "dropping by," but when I drop by I'm always made to feel that I'm intruding or interrupting something?*

If my mother in-law thinks it's okay for other people to drop by our place unannounced, she missed a sign somewhere. When I open my front door to a guest, or even my own mother, I like to be showered and dressed, with something more in my refrigerator than a carton of leftover fried rice. I don't know anyone who gets a kick out of being caught off guard.

How much fun is it to visit someone unexpectedly and have to stand there while they pick the dirty clothes and newspapers off the furniture so you have a place to sit down? What's the thrill in watching us scrape the bottom of a coffee can, looking for that last scoop that will barely make two cups?

I don't understand why this is even an issue. We don't think it's proper for anybody to just come by unexpectedly —especially in this day of car phones and cell phones. Why wouldn't you call first? There are pay phones on every corner in town. Mom, go for the phone call, next time you want to drop by.

Q: *Why is it my in-law child's mother can do whatever she likes in their house—go through drawers, hunt in closets, you name it—but when I open a cabinet to look for a spoon, I'm being nosy?*

Please understand that my mother has been going through my drawers for a lot of years. I've told her we don't like it and it's time to stop—and I'm ashamed to admit that she doesn't listen to me.

I don't think anyone has the right to rummage through someone else's bureau or closet or bathroom cabinet without permission. I don't need anyone knowing my bra size.

That goes for my mother, as well as my mother-in-law. I get really upset when someone does that, no matter whose mother she is.

We could use a little respect and privacy from both mothers. Are we asking too much?

Q: *Why does my daughter-in-law always take my grandchildren to her mother's home? She never brings them here to spend a day with me. It's not fair.*

My mother-in-law is right, it's *not* fair, but let me explain how this misunderstanding got started. Ever since the new baby was born, I feel as if I never get to see my mother enough. When I go over there, my intention is not to give her time with the baby — *I'm* trying to spend more time with my mother.

I only wish my husband would take the baby over to his mom's house more often and spend some time with *her*. But he feels I have to be with him when he goes to his mom's. I try to go, but when I can't, I think my husband should visit and take the baby by himself.

It's a shame he's not comfortable visiting his mother alone, and she ought to discuss it with *him*. I want her to see more of her grandchild, but I can't always be the one to do all the carting.

Q: *Why does my son think he has to listen to everything his wife says? He used to have a mind of his own. What happened?*

My husband *does* have a mind of his own — he just hates

using it. His mother hasn't lived with him for so long, she forgets that her son doesn't like to make decisions. At one time, he left the decision-making to her. Now he leaves it to me.

Does she think I'm a bossy wife? Maybe I am, but did my mother-in-law forget how many times she had to remind him to do something? If my mother-in-law feels that her son is being pushed around, I'm sorry. It's not true.

Q: *Why doesn't my son-in-law ever call me?*

Hey, I think my mother-in-law is the greatest, but the thought of calling her out of the blue just never crossed my mind. Is that wrong?

I mean, what am I going to say to her? The only thing we ever talk about is my wife or the kids. We do enough of that when I am with her.

I must admit I feel a little uncomfortable sometimes when she calls the house and tries to start a conversation with me. Don't misunderstand me—it's not her. I just don't think we have a helluva a lot we can discuss. It doesn't mean I don't like her.

You know, men don't usually make phone calls unless they have something to say. They don't just call up people to chat or hang on the phone for hours. Don't take it personally, Mom. It's a guy thing.

Q: *Why doesn't my son take charge of his kids? He goes along without saying anything about where they go and what they do.*

My mother-in-law has a right to think it's a shame that, after a hard day's work, her son has to drive the kids all over the place—play dates, soccer practice, the mall—as if he were a taxi service. Maybe she thinks the kids are getting spoiled and they should learn to do more things on their own. I'm aware that my mother-in-law feels my children are running wild. I can see the expression on her face and hear the disapproval in her voice whenever she asks what they're up to.

We've made tons of mistakes raising these kids. I'm not arguing about that. Maybe we should have listened to her a little more. But we're like all parents—we're learning how to do this job one day at a time. I feel as if I always have to defend myself because she doesn't accept the way we are raising our kids.

Instead of only focusing on what being a parent is doing to her son, I wish that just once she could see what it's doing to me too. And instead of feeling sorry for him every time he complains about running around, I wish she could see how much he really loves doing things for his kids.

Q: *Why is my in-law child cold to my other children?*

My mother-in-law and I get along just great. I feel bad that I don't have the same relationship with her other children, my in-laws.

My relationship with my brothers-in-law and sisters-in-law has nothing to do with her. It's not her fault and she can't fix it. I happen to be having some difficulties with them, and

I don't want to talk to her about it. But my mother-in-law doesn't seem to be able to accept this. By bringing it up and trying to smooth everything over, she's only causing more stress in an already uncomfortable situation.

Who knows? In time, her other children and I may be able to work out our differences. I hope my relationship with my mother-in-law is strong enough to stand on its own and that she has enough faith in all of us to let us work it out ourselves.

Q: *Why does my daughter-in-law run to tell my son whenever I've done something she doesn't like? Why doesn't she come and tell me?*

I didn't realize I was causing trouble for my mother-in-law. I always tell my husband all my complaints. I'm just letting off steam; I don't mean to make it a big deal.

When I tell my husband about something my mother or my friends at work have done that irked me, my husband would never dream of going back and telling them what I'd said. It didn't occur to me that he'd take it so seriously when I complained about his mother that he'd actually repeat it to her.

Why don't I tell my mother-in-law instead of him? That's obvious — the last thing I want is a confrontation with my mother-in-law. Sure, I get annoyed at her on occasion when I don't like something, but it doesn't mean I don't love her. Honestly, I'm not trying to make trouble. It's just me being me. Come on, Mom, lighten up a little.

Q: *When I phone my daughter-in-law, she always says she's busy and rushes me off. So how come when her family calls, suddenly she has time to stay on the phone for hours?*

It's not that I don't like my mother-in-law or don't find her interesting. But sometimes she just wants to hang on the phone without having very much to say. I don't feel comfortable making small talk. So far, all we actually have in common is her son. Maybe in time we will have more to talk about, but forcing a conversation is not a smart thing to do. It leads to gossiping or complaining, and I'm not comfortable with that. This is my husband's family we're talking about. My mother-in-law doesn't have to hear me bitching about how her son forgot to take out the trash again last night. I don't have to know what every last cousin is up to, either.

Sometimes I call her just to touch base or ask if everything is okay. I can tell she gets mad or feels insulted if I don't stay on with her for a long time. Don't you think that a short-but-good conversation is better than hanging on the phone for an hour saying nothing?

Q: *Whenever I discipline my grandchildren, my son-in-law tells me not to. That's his job, he says. So why, when his mother does it, is it okay? Why is she "teaching them manners" or "showing them how to behave" but I'm "interfering"?*

If my mother-in-law thinks I like it any better when my mother disciplines our children, she's mistaken. I don't like anyone telling my kids what to do. Maybe my mother-in-law has overheard my mother discipline my kids and thought I gave her permission. Believe me, she does it on her own, no matter what I tell her. Let's face facts. My mother doesn't care if I get angry at her. For obvious reasons, it rolls off her back. She does just what she pleases.

You know what's nice? My mother-in-law actually listens to me. I appreciate that she respects what I say. I know she feels bad if I get mad because she takes me more seriously than my mother does.

But you know what I don't get? Why would my mother-in-law want to discipline her grandchildren in the first place? Hasn't she had enough of bringing up kids? For heaven's sake, she should relax. She doesn't have to be their mother. When I get to be a grandfather, I'm going to have one rule. As soon as my grandchildren stop being fun, the night is over for me. I'm outa there. That's the luxury of being a grandparent. You hand the kids back to their mother and you say, "It's been a lovely evening. Good night."

My mother-in-law should just love and enjoy them. If they get to be too much to handle when she's watching them, don't watch them anymore. If they get out of hand while she's visiting at our house, go home. She deserves nothing but pleasure from being with her grandchildren.

Q: *Why is it that, during family affairs, my daughter-in-law talks only to her mother and never to me?*

My mother loves to talk and she always has my attention. I don't mean to leave my mother-in-law out. I try to bring her into the conversation, but it's hard sometimes. Nobody gets a word in edgewise with my mother. We don't even try anymore. How is my mother-in-law supposed to join in a conversation about Cousin Annie's latest plastic surgery? My mother-in-law doesn't know who Cousin Annie is. Sometimes, I'm not sure *I* know which one Cousin Annie is.

I enjoy my mother-in-law's company when my mother is not around. My mother-in-law doesn't demand my attention nearly as much as my mother does, thank heavens. How do I convey that to my mother-in-law without running down my own mother?

I have my hands full when I have to entertain both my husband's mother and my own. I am very uncomfortable when they are together, but there's not much I can do about it. Mother-in-law, I could use a little understanding at times like this. My mom gives me enough trouble as it is.

Q: *Whenever my daughter-in-law's mother suggests which wallpaper to use in the kitchen or where to go on vacation, she says her mother has great ideas. Whenever I suggest something, my son calls me to the side and tells me to butt out. Why?*

It's not fair that my husband is so strict with his own mother. If her son calls her to the side to tell her something like that, she should take it up with him. I've never asked him to do that and I never would.

I'm sorry my mother-in-law feels her ideas aren't valued. It's just that when I lived at home, my mother and I always shopped together and decorated the house together. I have relied on my mother's taste for years and just didn't feel it necessary to ask my mother-in-law's opinion. I feel so bad that she takes this personally, and I didn't mean to offend her. This is just what I'm used to.

Q: *When I give my daughter-in-law money, she thanks me and puts it away in the bank. I know she does the same thing with her mother. The difference is that when I go back three weeks later, she's showing off something she bought with the money her mother gave her. What did they do with the money I gave her, use it to buy compost?*

I have always appreciated my mother-in-law's cash gifts, because I always felt we could do with them what we pleased and she wouldn't care. On the other hand, my mother insists that I buy something she thinks we need, and then I have to show it to her. It makes me feel a little childish, but that's the way my mother is.

I had no idea that my mother-in-law kept such a close eye on the gifts she gave us. I think that's great. I will pay more attention the next time she gives us money. If my mother in-law wants me to buy something and show it to her, from now on I will. Sorry, Mom, I wasn't hiding anything from you. I didn't know it mattered to you.

Q: *Why does my in-law child's family get better and more expensive gifts than I do?*

This is going to seem crazy, but I try to spend the same amount on other people as they spend on me. Let me see if I can explain it. My mother always gives me and my husband more expensive gifts than my mother-in-law usually does. That's understandable because, financially, my family is a little better off. Maybe that is not the way I should buy gifts, but it's the way I've shopped for presents all my life. I'm sorry that my shopping system made my mother-in-law think I'm treating my family more special or that I didn't care about her. I never intended that.

Q: *Why is my son-in-law's mother allowed to worry and talk about her problems as much as she wants? When I have a problem, I'm not allowed to talk about it when I'm with them.*

If my mother-in-law feels that we're not listening to her problems or that we're bored by them, she's wrong. We want very much to help her, or at least take her mind off them. But when we try to help, we aren't much use. It makes us feel as if nothing we do can make a difference. What she mistakes for annoyance is our frustration.

We feel the same way about my mother, but I've been dealing with my mother a lot longer. So if my mother-in-law thinks that I seem more sympathetic to my mom, tell my mother-in-law that all she's seeing is many years' worth of conditioning. I would never want her to feel that we don't care about her if she's got troubles.

Q: *When they come to visit me, my married children are in and out of the house so fast I feel as if I live in a hamburger drive-through. Why do they do that?*

Usually, my mother-in-law just asks us to stop by. So if

we sometimes seem to be in and out in a hurry, it's because that's the way we thought she wanted it. We feel as if we're putting her out because she thinks she has to entertain us.

She always seems to be preoccupied or too busy to sit with us. She's involved in what's going on with everyone else in the family. We come to visit to be with her. Instead, we have to hear about the rest of the family, and we can't seem to get through an entire conversation about ourselves.

If we thought she wanted us to come and relax and just spend the day, of course we'd spend more time with her. I'd be happy to have dinner or lunch with her when the time is right; all she would have to do is call and invite us. It's no problem for us.

Q: *Why is it that, when my son-in-law comes to my house, he either sits in front of the TV watching football as if my house were a sports bar or lies on the couch and conks out like a beached whale?*

I guess my mother-in-law thinks I should be different in her house than I am in my own home or my mother's home. Lord knows, she causes enough fights between me and my wife to let me know she doesn't like it.

My wife understands that I'm just looking to relax, but her mother gives her such a hard time about it. Why does my mother-in-law think that if I don't sit at the table all day with the rest of the family—listening to everyone talk about people I hardly know—that I'm being rude or disrespectful? I wish she would realize this is my day off and I'm doing my own thing. No skin off her nose, right? I don't mean to offend or hurt anyone's feelings.

The irony is that I love to go to my mother-in-law's house. She's a great cook and a nice woman. I just want her to see that I'm trying to relax and enjoy the day too. Please, Mom, give me a little (nap) break.

10

Whose Baby Is This Anyway?

YOU CAN'T blame first-time grandmothers. In all the tumult and anticipation, it's easy to get carried away. At the first word that her married kids are going to have a baby, a mother-in-law wants to jump into the excitement and confusion with both feet. Then she gets hurt when she discovers there's no room in the pool for her.

It's amazing how many mothers-in-law forget what it was like when they were pregnant. Remember being frantic with fifty thousand decisions that had to be made before the baby arrived? Not to mention the constant worry. Put yourself back there for a moment, and feel the anxiety your married children must be feeling. Can they afford this new child? Will they need more room? Is her husband ready for a baby? Is *she* ready? Should they have saved for a house first? How will the other children adjust to the new baby? How are they going to afford college for the child? Heck, have you seen what *preschool* costs these days?

It's a trying time. but don't worry. When the baby finally comes, there will be plenty for you to do. Until then, satisfy yourself with all the things a grandmother-to-be could want to do. Call every friend and relative in your phone book and give them the good news. Call a press conference if you want. Call the admissions office at Princeton. Let loose and celebrate, but tread softly around your married children. This is their time, their moment. Let them star.

Lots of married children will want to discuss baby names with their mothers-in-law as the due date gets closer. Some even seek out their mothers-in-law for advice about prenatal care. Others are grateful their mothers-in-law can stay with them for a week or two after the baby is born. But there's no law that says they must do these things. If your in-law child wants to talk names with you, go ahead. If they want your advice on doctors, hospitals, medical care, give them the benefit of your vast experience. If they need you to stay with them (and you want to do it), who's stopping you? But you can't volunteer any of these things unless you are asked. Be cool—ahead of you is an entire lifetime, the life of your new grandchild. You'll be needed soon enough.

When your married children are pregnant, the most precious thing, you'll find, will be useful information. They have it; you want it. You're going to be tempted to torture them for the slightest news. How does she feel today? What did the sonogram show? Is it a boy? Think she'll really deliver by the due date? Your married children know how concerned you are and that you're a walking wheelbarrow full of questions. They love you and they'll get around to answering all of them—in time. Just give them a chance.

If it's your daughter-in-law who is pregnant, don't take

offense that her mother knows about new developments before you do. Girls talk more to their mothers than boys do. The other mother is bound to find out some things faster than you, so accept it. This isn't a contest, and for Pete's sake don't accuse your daughter-in-law of keeping secrets if your son forgets to share some small piece of news.

If your daughter is having the baby, remind her to include *her* mother-in-law in the circle for news. In fact, try to include the other mother yourself.

Having a baby shower? Give your in-law child's mother the chance to help in the plans and preparation if she wants to join in. Suggest that the two of you go shopping together for baby furniture, clothes, whatever. Perhaps the two of you can volunteer to get the baby's room ready. I can think of nothing more wonderful than two grandmothers working together to help out their children.

If the other mother lives out of town, call her once in a while just to talk or give her an update. Even if it's news she already knows, it's a comfort to hear someone else say it. If you have the room, invite her to stay with you for the birth. Your son-in-law will love any thoughtful thing you can do for his parents during this time.

Anxious or excited? Don't call your kids. Instead call your counterpart, the other grandmother, and talk to her about it. Together, the two of you can channel all that raging, grandmother energy into each other. Everyone involved should be made to feel special. But don't expect your eight-and-a-half-months-pregnant daughter or your son-in-law to pay much attention to you or the other parents. This is a time when grandparents should take care of one another.

If you want to help, there are just two rules you need to follow:

1. Leave all the decisions to them.
2. Agree with all the decisions they make, even if you hate them.

That's as easy to remember as your own name, isn't it? All the decisions are theirs to make, and you're going to love (or pretend to love) all of them.

Do you feel you just *have* to do more? Okay, here's a list of things you can do to make things easier for your married children, who—by the way—are the ones you should be thinking about right now.

~ Send them pot roasts, fried chicken, lasagna, tofu burgers —whatever their favorite dinners are—so she doesn't have to cook.
~ Give her a day out. Treat her to nails, hair, a facial, anything to make her feel good.
~ Run some errands for her.
~ Take her kids to school one day or pick them up after school for an afternoon at your house. Take them for the entire weekend, if their mother agrees.
~ Drive her to her doctor's visit.
~ Buy her something very pretty.

~ Take or send flowers.
~ Remind your son to do things that make her feel special.
~ Send her funny greeting cards now and then.
~ Take her out to dinner. Just her.
~ Pay her *lots* of compliments.
~ Make a lunch for her and her friends, her sisters, or her family.
~ Buy her some books to read.
~ Get her CDs or tapes of some of her favorite music.
~ Make sure she gets a chance to rest when she comes to visit you.

There's so much you can do that reinforces your place in the lives of your married children—without taking over their lives. Here are some bad ideas for mothers-in-law to do, things you should avoid pretty much at all costs.

~ Don't *always* talk about the baby. It's going to be a long nine months. Change the subject every now and then.
~ Don't try to explain every pain or unusual feeling she has.
~ Don't keep mentioning how big she's getting.
~ Don't tell her what to eat and what to avoid.
~ Don't keep telling her she needs bigger maternity clothes.
~ Don't tell her that her face is changing.
~ Don't stay late when you visit.

Most important of all, don't tell her childbirth horror stories. A young friend's mother-in-law drove her crazy during her pregnancy with stories of babies born with not enough fingers or too many toes. The dreadful stories never stopped: tales of women who were in labor for days on end, obstetricians who didn't show up in time, babies switched in the hospital. "Every time my mother-in-law left my house, I was awake all night," this friend recalled. "She just had this perverse need to tell me about everything that could go wrong."

It's very easy to get caught up in the excitement of your daughter having a baby, so try not to lose sight of your son-in-law. A pregnancy is no excuse for nightly invasions of his home. If you're calling ten times a day for up-to-the-minute bulletins or constantly dropping by their house to check that she's all right, he is bound to start wondering, Doesn't my mother-in-law think I'm capable of taking care of my wife?

Every time you say your daughter shouldn't be doing certain things—driving, climbing ladders, eating chili—he's got to be fuming, 'Doesn't she think I'm paying attention to my wife?' Every time he's pushed aside, he's sputtering, 'Who's having this baby anyway, my wife and I—or my mother-in-law and her daughter?'

Every now and then, make *him* feel like the special one, instead of always fussing over your daughter. His wife is going through more changes, emotionally and physically, than either of them ever imagined—and he's the one who has to deal with it. Making him a favorite meal, picking up something nice for him before you drop by, are some of the things you can do that will make him see that you also realize what he's going through. If you want to preserve your welcome at your kids' home, pay plenty of attention to the father-to-be.

22

A Guide for Grandmothers

*T*HERE'S A SECRET to getting the love and attention you have earned from your grandchildren. Here it is: look after their parents. That's right. If you want to be a happy grandmother, your married children hold the keys to the kingdom.

Too many grandmothers learn this fact the hard way. Sometimes I marvel at how hardheaded mothers-in-law can be. How can they bicker with their married children week after week and then expect to have the simple, unspoiled love of their grandchildren? Do they actually believe there is no connection between parents and their children?

Now that you are a grandmother, your obligation is not just to your new grandchild. It's your job to take care of and support your married children in the amazingly difficult job of bringing up their kids. If you can do it with a smile and an open heart, everything else you want and desire for your grandchildren will fall into place.

You may have been the perfect mother-in-law up to this point. You stayed out of the wedding plans. You don't visit without an invitation. You don't take sides in their disputes. You know and understand your place.

Now that there are grandchildren in the picture, don't forget who you are. You are the parent's parent—that doesn't give you parental rights. If they want the baby to be born at home or in a birthing center or at a Sunoco station, that's where the baby is going to be born. If they want to let their little boy's hair grow down to his waist, that's their business.

What's more important, that your grandchild wear his hair the way you think he should or that you are a welcome part of your grandchild's life? Think about it. As a grandmother, you can play an irreplaceable role in the lives of your kids' kids. Don't get shut out.

Your grandchildren have parents who lay down the rules and deserve to be respected. If you need an incentive or reminder, try this: Your grandchildren will be happier, grow up stronger, smarter, and more secure, if you take care of their parents with the same love and concern you lavish on them.

Step one, teach your in-law children not to be too hard on themselves and make sure they take some time together. Help them to understand that doing what they think is right is the only guiding light a parent has.

It's important to your married children to have support from someone who truly matters to them. Sometimes, just knowing that you are in their corner is enough to get them through. Make sure they always know that you are there for them. Tell them how hard they are working and what a good job of parenting they're doing. They need to hear it from you.

Here's some other guidance on how to hold up your end of the bargain.

1. On those nights you are baby-sitting, try to go to their home. You can make your married children's life a lot easier if they don't have to lug equipment wherever they go. Moving a child from place to place these days can require the kind of planning the Allies did at Normandy for D day: car seats, strollers, toys, diapers, food, warmers, and coolers. Cut down on the confusion and go to their place.

2. If your grandchildren are staying with you, however, offer to keep the kids overnight if their parents want. Whenever they choose to pick up their children and take them home, let them. No whining, no fussing from you.

3. In two-income households, grandparents often play a big role as caretakers. The good grandmother doesn't bring to her children's attention all the things she's doing for them — and what others don't do. She does what she has to and keeps quiet about it.

4. Tell stories to your grandchildren about their other grandparents. "When you had your first birthday, Grandma Marie and I decorated the house for your party. We filled all the tables with balloons. We took pictures of you and your friends. We had such fun. We love doing things for you." Imagine how your in-law child will feel, hearing you tell a story like that. Your grandchild will love it too. What a secure feeling it is for a child to know that everyone they love, also loves the others.

5. If you're taking the kids out, make sure it's a convenient time for your in-law child, not just you. Are you demanding to take the kids on weekends, when your married

children want to be together as a family? Or are you always busy on the weekends when your married children would most appreciate an offer to take the kids for a little while? If you're going to do someone a favor, make sure it's really a favor.

You don't have to have all the answers. When your in-law child complains about the kids, just try to listen. Most times, he or she is not looking for answers anyway but just wants to let off steam, so relax and lend an ear for a while.

In tough spots, encourage your married children to seek professional help.

When they come to your house, treat your married children as specially as you do your grandkids. If you bought goodies for the kids, why not goodies for their father or mother as well? Grandchildren love seeing their parents get gifts too.

Young children will try to put you in the middle of their arguments with their parents, but don't let it happen. If your grandchild gets angry at your son-in-law or daughter-in-law, *never* speak against the parents. No one says you have to take sides in these disagreements, so try to say nothing; it's very effective. As a rule, grandchildren hate to displease their grandparents, and your silence will let them know you aren't happy with them. (It also gives quiet support to your in-law child.) Or try saying, "Grandma's job of making decisions is over. Grandma Marie and I both taught Mommy and Daddy the right thing to do. I doubt your parents would do anything to hurt you."

Sooner or later, kids will also try to go over their parents' heads to their grandparents. Kids and their grandparents form a natural alliance against the authority of the parents. After all, grandparents aren't intimidated by Mommy and Daddy. Together, grandmother and grandchild create a secret bond based on opposition to the parents. "Here's five dollars. Put it away and don't tell your father." Or "Grandma, I can stay up till eleven to watch TV, can't I? Mommy doesn't have to know."

No one is going to deny you a $5 bill every now and then. But once you make that secret pact with your grandchildren, you're telling them it's okay to sneak around, perhaps even to lie to their parents. You have begun to undercut your own position too. Don't underestimate the important part you play in raising your grandchild right.

Part of your job is teaching your grandchildren responsibility when they're away from home. Just because they are out of their parents' sight doesn't mean they should be allowed to leave the rules at home. What's a little cup of ice cream to a child? Nothing, really. But it's *not* the cup of ice cream that counts. It's minding the parents' rules.

Here's a place where you can be a true help to your married children. What do the grandchildren think when their grandmother won't obey their parents? If you won't, why should they? "Oh, Grandma, I'll finish studying for my test in the morning. Let me watch the end of this movie." What's the big deal, asks Grandmother? All by themselves, they're not big deals. But by letting your grandchildren stay up longer than they're allowed, you just taught them that defiance is all right as long as no one finds out. Grandparents tend to think their married children are punishing them when they get mad over a forbidden ice-cream cone or a missed bedtime. It's not about you, Grandma, it's about Junior.

Sure, parents (especially first-time parents) sometimes overreact. But that's their right too. If they don't want your grandchild drinking soda or wolfing down chocolate bars, you must respect that: no soda and no Snickers at Grandma's house.

Are they trying to raise the first American child in fifty years who doesn't know what a television set is? Well, then, the kid shouldn't be sneaking TV time at your home. No war toys? Then pass right by the aisle with the six-shooters at Toys "Я" Us. Don't think you'll be able to do something they won't approve of and then set things right later. If your married children have rules about their kids, no matter how uptight they seem, try your best to back them up.

When in doubt about whether your children will approve of where you're taking the kids or what you may be doing with them, ask. The important thing is not to surprise them. In fact, make that your motto: No surprises. Let your married children know what you're doing at every step.

This way you stay out of trouble, which is good for everyone. Youngsters abhor seeing their parents fight with their grandparents. When you cross the boundaries that your married children set up for their kids, you never know what the ramifications will be.

Every grandmother wants to say yes to her grandchildren and every parent has to say no a couple of million times in the course of raising a child. Help your married children say "no" when it's necessary—and every time you want to be with your grandchildren, their answer will be yes.

23

What Your Grandchildren Really Want

GRANDCHILDREN WANT you to love them, of course. But they want you to love their mothers and father just as much. To some mothers-in-law, this idea may actually be news.

They tend to think they can maintain a close, nurturing relationship with their grandchildren at the same time they are battling with their own children. Kids, especially young ones, see their families as one unit, inseparable and whole. Bad times in one corner of the family overshadows the sunshine everywhere else.

To test this idea that children are acutely aware of the ways in which their grandparents treat their own parents, I asked a bunch of children in my family and the children of friends, "What do you want your grandmother to do for your mommy? Or daddy?" and I inserted the name of the grandmother's in-law child.

Not one child said "nothing." They all quickly volunteered suggestions, and in most cases the answers were wonderfully appropriate to their ages. Here's a sample of their responses. Remember, these are kids talking about how they'd like to see you treat your in-law children.

- "I would like my nanny to go to work for my father every day, so he can stay home and rest his bad knee." — *Louis Roggeman, 5*
- "I would like my nanny to come to my house and help my father when my mother fights and picks on him." — *Tori Roggeman, 10*
- "I would like my nanny to take my mother to the movies and buy her candy — just like she does with me." — *Bianca Giordano, 7*
- "My mother loves to take care of little dogs. I would like my nanny and my mother to go into business together taking care of the dogs for people. I think that they would do good in business and make a lot of money." — *Ruthie Russo, 9*
- "I would like my nanny and my mother to hang out together. Just be friends." — *Frankie Russo, 15*
- "We want our nanny to buy our father season tickets to the Yankees." — *Tomi Lee, 13, and Natalie Cespuglio, 15*
- "I would like my grandmother to treat my mother just like she treats me, special. I would love to see her treat my mother like a daughter." — *Jennifer Giordano, 11*
- "I want my nanny to come and help my father when her daughter gets unreasonable and gives him a difficult time." — *Ann Nicole Stanco, 13*

~ "I wish my grandma could come to my house and cook something special for my father." —*Julianne Carlucci, 10*

~ "I wish my grandma could come to my house when my mother comes home from work and do the cooking for her. That way, my mother just has to do the wash."— *Katharine Forte, 10*

~ "I just want my nanny to love my mother and come to my house and help her out because she works late."— *Melissa Giordano, 15*

~ "I want Grandma to come to the house and read my mother a book." —*Leo Mancini, 3*

~ "My mother works six days a week, and on her only day off, she has to clean the house and do all the wash for my whole family. I wish that on my mother's day off, my grandmother could come and help her so she can get some time for herself."—*Sejin Kim, 12*

~ "I want Grandma to come to my house and bake a cake for my mommy and put whipped cream on it for her."— *Kristy Rae Dice, 3*

~ "I know she can't, but I wish my grandmother would go to work instead of my mother for about a month. That way my mother could stay home and rest." —*Lauren Heidinger, 14*

~ "Even though my parents are divorced, I like it when my grandma shows my mother respect, when she asks me how she is and things like that."—*Alexis Stuono, 14*

~ "I want my *abuela* to give my mother a big surprise party for her fiftieth birthday." —*Richard Rosario, 10*

~ "I want my grandmother to give my mother all her money because my mother loves money." — *Tara Maria D'Aleo, 10*

Kids are remarkably tuned in to the burdens of being a parent. We tend to assume they are lost in the TV or games and are oblivious to what's going on with us. Nothing could be further from the truth. They know how hard we work and how aggravating making a living and taking care of a family can be. Even at an early age, children seem to understand that adults need to relax ("I want Grandma to come to the house and read my mother a book"). Not so surprising really; we tell them often enough. "Honey, go play with Daddy. Mommy's tired."

Of course, young kids are self-centered, but they have sensitive radar for what the weather is like in the rest of the family. Don't think for a moment you can hide from them.

We figure that as long as everything is good between grandma and grandchild, that's all that matters. If only that were true. Your grandchildren want you to love your in-law child as much as you love them.

24

A Few Good Deeds, Well Done

I T TOOK ME three marriages to realize how unusual it is for a mother-in-law to see her in-law children as individuals, separate and distinct from their own children. More to the point, it took three wedding showers for me to see it.

It was my mother-in-law Elaine whose gift stole the show at my last wedding shower. She gave me a gorgeous, quite distinctive, *very* elegant gold bracelet. I got a lot of beautiful presents that day, including a bedroom set and a California honeymoon. But after the gifts had been opened, it was the bracelet that all my friends and family huddled to see. What was the commotion about?

It was the fact that Elaine had given a present just for me. Not that I didn't like the trip or furniture, but they were for both of us. This was a present *for me*.

My new mother-in-law had sent a special message that day. She was telling me that, in her eyes, I would be more than just her son's wife. She was going to treat me as an independent person, a member of her family, someone who would get attention for being who she was. All that from a bracelet.

A lot of mothers-in-law want to treat their in-law children special but don't know how. I hear it all the time. "I ask my daughter-in-law what she wants for her birthday, and she always says the same thing. 'Don't make a fuss. Something little.' It's the same thing with my son-in-law, but he says 'No, don't bother.' It's very frustrating."

If these answers sound familiar, here are some special things you can do on their birthdays or holidays or just to make them feel better. These are gestures, big and small, that don't require their cooperation but show your in-law child how much you care.

~ Throw a party and invite *their* friends. No uncles, aunts, or friends of yours; strictly a guest list of their own choosing without family obligation. I know a mother-in-law who, with her daughter, made a men's-only supper at her house for her son-in-law. They cooked, set the table, and then left. When his friends arrived, they had a night of steak, cigars, and brandy. Just the guys. He never forgot it. Another friend threw her daughter-in-law a birthday party at her summer house. She told her married children to ask whomever they wanted, made a grand meal for the whole crowd, and invited them all to stay overnight. The party went on for two days. It was a memorable event.

~ When you go visiting, pick up something he likes: wine, golf balls, fishing lures, a computer game, wrist bands, jogging pants, whatever. But don't worry about getting the wrong wine or the wrong computer game. Mothers-in-law end up buying shirts and sweaters for their sons-in-law because they don't know what else to get. Ask around what his favorite things might be. You want to show that you put more stock in your in-law child than what Van Heusen has to offer.

~ Buy her some pretty writing paper with her name embossed on it.

~ Inviting your married children out to dinner? Take him to his favorite restaurant, some place *he* wants to go—not you.

~ Pick up her favorite perfume for no damn reason, just as a token.

~ Is your son-in-law proud of how well he cooks? When he comes to your house, why not put the spatula in his hand? Or ask him to make a special dish for one of your parties. If he really enjoys cooking, he'll be flattered.

~ Going out with your married children? Let him drive or, better yet, give him the keys to your car. It lets him know that it's okay with you for him to be in charge.

~ Your in-law child has his or her heart set on a big-ticket item—a car, a computer, going back to school. Offer to contribute to the cause. Don't be put off if you can't pay for the whole thing. You're only looking to help out, so show them that you care and get them started with a down payment or one semester. You want to be a friend, not a benefactor.

~ On your in-law child's birthday, send flowers or a basket to his or her mother with a note saying thanks for raising such a beautiful kid—and how lucky you are that your child found them both.

25

Getting to Know You

WE ALL HAVE the need to be recognized and sin-gled out. We want to know in our hearts that we are unique in the eyes of the people we love. I put recognition right up there on the scale of human needs with food, shelter, and belly laughs.

If you can recognize and respect your in-law children, you won't believe the attention they give you back. Once they get the recognition they crave from you, they'll do just about anything to keep it—and you—in their lives.

But you can't give a person recognition without knowing what you're recognizing them for. First you may have to do some homework. This probably sounds obvious, but your in-law children have their own lives, separate and apart from your children. They have their own separate histories, hopes, and dreams.

So what are their talents, their values, their political thoughts? What do they take pride in? What—or whom—do they hate? What are they really passionate about? Ask yourself: Who is my daughter-in-law (or son-in-law) and what do I know about her—besides what I learned from talking to her about my son? What are her hopes for the future? Where does she see herself twenty years from now?

Too many mothers-in-law can't answer these basic questions. It takes time and energy to get to know their in-law children. To some, the son-in-law is just the chauffeur who drops their daughter off to see them on Saturdays; the daughter-in-law is the woman who takes care of their grandchildren between visits to Grandma.

Men and women seek recognition in very different ways. Women want to be listened to — that makes them feel respected. Men, on the other hand, want to feel they are needed and useful. They want to know they can do things others cannot. That's what makes them feel respected.

Start building recognition with your son-in-law by asking his advice about something. Which car to buy? Who makes the best outdoor grill? What should you plant in the garden next year? What's the difference between two mutual funds? If you can, avoid asking him something he doesn't know anything about. Remember, he wants you to think he's sharp.

Start by phoning your daughter-in-law once a week or so. Call at a time of day when your son is not home so she knows you are calling for her. Talk about anything *except* her kids and your son. For many mothers-in-law, these are the only topics of conversation they ever seem to discuss with their daughters-in-law. It's not surprising because these are the biggest things they have in common — until they begin to establish a relationship of their own.

So what do you talk about to break the ice? Begin by asking about her family. Be specific.

"Is your Aunt Helen home from the hospital?"

"How did your brother's graduation go?"

Ask questions that will elicit her feelings, her opinions, or her advice.

"I'm having a problem with a neighbor. You're fair-minded. What do you think I should do?"

"My boss expects me to do the work that used to be done by two people. Do you think I should change jobs?"

Remember, women want to be heard, so when she begins answering, be sure to restrain the urge to offer your opinion. Just listen for now. In the beginning, let your daughter-in-law talk for as long as she likes and pay attention to what she has to say. You are like a bank; and every time your in-law child tells you something personal, she is making a deposit into an account. By being a patient listener, you make her feel that her account is safe with you. Don't worry, your turn to talk will come.

If you're like most mothers-in-law, you've spent hours telling her all the old family stories about what your kids did when they were growing up — first broken arms, most embarrassing moments, and so on. But have you shared anything of yourself with them? In time, your son-in-law or daughter-in-law will be curious to learn the important things about you.

Now is your moment to talk about your hopes and concerns. Does getting older bother you? What did you hope to do in life but never got around to? What did you want to grow up to be when you were little? What are your dreams for retirement? What do you hope for your children? Make sure to include your in-law children in those dreams. That's the way you make someone part of your family. *That's* recognition.

26

In Praise of Praise

Y NOW, you should know a bit more about what makes your son-in-law or daughter-in-law tick. Here is how to put that knowledge to use. After recognizing who they are as individuals, it's time to acknowledge them And how do you do that? One word—praise.

Praise them to the heavens and back. Praise them by day, praise them by night, praise them until your lips fall off. If your appreciation is sincere, you cannot overdo it.

There are two types of praise.

1. Tell your son-in-law or daughter-in-law directly what a good person you think they are.
2. Tell others—in the presence of your in-law child—how much you think of the person your son or daughter married.

Brag about something your son-in-law does, other than what he does for a living. Tell him how much you love how he plays the guitar, or how he should have been a sportswriter because he knows so much about football. Don't hesitate to mention a kind or thoughtful thing your daughter-in-law did lately. "Peggy baby-sat for her neighbor's children last weekend so the parents could get away for a while."

Tell your son-in-law he's going to make a good father—or, if he already has children, what a good father he is. Repeat the stories his children tell about him. "Your son said you're teaching him how to swim. He loves you to death. You're such a good father."

Notice new clothes or new haircuts. Say how nice he looks.

Talk about how special your son-in-law or daughter-in-law treats your parents. "My father is crazy for my son-in-law. Grandpa loves young people, and my son-in-law always gives him special attention. They talk about the old baseball players. My father thinks the world of my son-in-law."

Whenever you get a gift from your in-law children, say how generous and thoughtful they are. If it's the wrong size, color, or model, don't say so. Give them credit for trying.

Brag about a speech your daughter-in-law gave at a business conference or a promotion she just got.

You've been around long enough to find something to praise—even if it doesn't come to mind right away.

If your son-in-law is cheap, tell him his thriftiness will help him and your daughter in the future. If he's a spendthrift, tell him how lucky your daughter is to be married to a generous man.

If he's late for dinner, sympathize with how busy he must be. If he's on time, tell him he was raised well by his parents and never keeps people waiting.

If he doesn't say much, call him "deep." If he won't shut up, call him "the life of the party."

If your daughter-in-law is smart, tell her how pretty she is. If she's pretty, tell her how smart she is.

Best of all, tell your son-in-law or daughter-in-law how lucky your child was to find such a good husband or good wife.

Don't be disheartened if your in-law children don't respond immediately. Give them time. They've known you only for a short while. Sooner or later, they'll start giving back all the attention and recognition you are giving them. Promise.

27

All the Ways to Support Your Kids

STANDING BEHIND your married children and the decisions they make is some of the toughest work you'll ever do, because it requires that you repress your own misgivings and doubts. Holding back those second thoughts can ruin the lining of your stomach and make you look old before your time. But it's one of the greatest gifts you can give them. Thankfully, that's not the only type of support you have to offer your married children.

There are some subtle side-door types of support you can give that will let them know how much you love and respect them. I'm talking about the kinds of things that take the pressure off and make it easier for them to love and respect you back. You have always tried to make the lives of your children easier; why stop now?

Let Them Off the Hook

Be the first one at a family affair to give your kids permission to go home early. How about saying, "You two don't have to stick around if you don't want to. I know you have a big day tomorrow and it's been a long evening." That's a sincere act of kindness.

So what if your son-in-law can't come to your birthday party because he has tickets to the ball game? Does he have to be at *every* family function? Don't get upset if your daughter-in-law has to go to a good-bye party for a friend at work and will miss your sister's anniversary. Maybe the problem is that you dread the moment when your sister asks, "So, where's your son and his wife?" What do you say? Try replying, "I don't know. Did you speak with them?" Those tickets and that good-bye party are every bit as important to your in-law children as your sister's anniversary is to you. You aren't required to make excuses for them.

Is your in-law child on a diet for medical reasons or just to slim down? Offer support. Ask, before they come over, "Is there anything special I can make for you? Do you need the blender? What can I get you?" Don't be the pushy mother-in-law, shoving food across the table at them, scolding them about how it's a special occasion or "just this once." No one is asking you to be the food police either, just be a little sensitive.

The harshest test of your ability to let your married children off the hook comes when they decide to move out of town. Maybe it's a job transfer or a new career opportunity. It may be a decision to move closer to your in-law child's family. They're probably going to be excited about moving to a new town, so don't take it the wrong way. They're not excited to be moving away from you. They're every bit as uncertain and anxious about this big change in their lives as you are. It's up to you to help by taking the pressure off them. Try telling them that after they move you'll have a new place to go for vacation.

Give a Helping Hand at the Right Moment

Are your married children struggling financially? Are there luxuries they can't afford? You can help out in little ways that will make a big difference. Pick up a couple of theater tickets for them. Send them out alone for a night on the town, rather than dragging them out with you. Treat them to a romantic dinner—just the two of them. You can arrange in advance with the restaurant to pay the bill with your credit card.

Respect a Confidence

If your in-law child tells you something in confidence, honor and respect that confidence by not repeating it to anyone. This may sound obvious—and it may not even strike you as being particularly supportive. But there is no greater way to build trust than to demonstrate that whatever you are told will go no further. How many mothers-in-law think, "It won't hurt if I tell my husband or my best friend"? Oh, yes, it will.

If your in-law child is having trouble with his or her family or having problems at work, don't think it was easy to confide in you. It's an act of trust. Betray that confidence just once, and it will take years (if ever) for your in-law child to trust you again.

Look the Other Way

If your married children are fighting, be like the three monkeys: hear nothing, see nothing, say nothing. Stay away until it blows over.

Did your son or daughter marry into a funny family? You know what I mean: Are they different from what you are used to? Are they from a culture you are unfamiliar with? Do they have a famous relative? Are they gamblers or sideshow performers or political radicals from the sixties? Is his mother an ex–Hollywood madam? Did his father run off with the baby-sitter?

If so, do your best to stay away from the subject. Leave the ball in your son-in-law or daughter-in-law's court. If they want to talk about where the circus is performing next week or how the case is going, let them raise the subject. Curiosity may be eating at you, but try to keep it in check. Nothing is more intrusive than being questioned about some subject you'd rather not talk about. In that type of situation, looking the other way qualifies as an act of love.

28

When to Call Your In-Law Child

- When there is illness on the in-law side of the family, a "What-can-I-do-for-you?" call wouldn't hurt.
- When she has to take a test, call to say good luck.
- When he gets a promotion, call to congratulate him.
- When they threw a great party, call the next day to say how wonderful it was.
- When he isn't feeling well, call to ask if he needs anything.
- When she helped you with a big dinner, call to thank her again the next day and tell her how easy she made things for you.
- When he showed unusual respect for someone in your family—like sending flowers to a sick relative—call to say how thoughtful he was.
- When she runs errands for you when you are sick, call to say how grateful you are.
- When he drives you somewhere, call later on to say thanks again.
- When they invite you to spend a weekend, call when you get home to tell them what a nice time you had.

~ When they spent a weekend at your home, call to tell them how much you enjoyed having them.

~ When they sent you a beautiful birthday card, call to thank them for thinking of you.

~ When they give you a present for the holidays, a thank-you call will say you don't take things like that for granted.

~ When she let you borrow her husband for a whole day to do some chore for you, call to say how generous it was of her to share him.

~ When he passes a course, call to recognize his accomplishment.

~ When she gave you something she was wearing because you had admired it, call to say she is one of a kind.

~ When someone in her family passes away, be the first one to call.

~ When they made their kids do something nice for you, call to say how lucky the children are to have them for parents.

~ When she went with you on a doctor's visit, call to tell her how special it made you feel.

~ When she wrote down a recipe for you, call after you make the dish to tell her how great it was.

~ When he does something nice for someone close to you —your husband, your son, or your father, for instance— call the next day to say thanks and let him know he is considered part of your family.

~ When she helped you around your house, call to tell her that having her is like having a daughter.
~ When her husband is away on a business trip, a call to ask her if everything is all right wouldn't hurt.
~ When you spot a sale at her favorite department store, call to tell her that now is her chance.
~ When someone on the in-law side of the family has done well, call to acknowledge the achievement.

29

When Never to Call Your In-Law Child

~ When it's the kids' bedtime, don't call. Remember how hard it was to get them settled in at night?

~ When she has failed at something, goofed up, or is feeling bad, don't call. She'll call you when she feels better.

~ When they are trying to make a big decision, don't call. Give them some room.

~ When they are having trouble on the job, don't call. Let things settle down.

~ When she is waiting for an important call, don't call. She'll let you know how things turned out.

~ When she has a falling out with a good friend, don't call; when she does call to talk about it, just listen.

~ When your in-law child is fighting with someone in your family—one of your children or another in-law child, for instance—don't call.

~ When they have had some disappointing news, don't call right away. Give it a chance to sink in.

~ When she is having problems with her kids, don't call. If she needs help, she'll holler.

~ When it's dinnertime, don't call, especially if they have young children.

~ When it's a weekend night after 10 P.M., don't call. This is the only real time they can stay up late together. Whatever you have to say can wait until morning.

~ When it's a weekend morning, try not to call before noon. This is the only real time they can hang out in bed together or just enjoy a quiet breakfast.

~ When you want to go over for a visit but aren't sure you can make it, don't call unless you are sure you can stop by. Ever plan around someone coming over, but they never show up?

~ When she is trying to study, don't call.

~ When he is working out, don't call.

~ When you are fighting with someone else in your family, don't call. Is it really necessary to put your kids in the middle?

~ When you are depressed, don't call—unless you're ready to listen to their advice or let them help you.

~ When you know they are entertaining, don't call. They've got their hands full.

~ When you just want to complain, don't call. They have their own problems.

30

Cheatin' Hearts

ARE YOU carrying around an awful secret? Do you suspect your in-law child is having an extramarital affair? It breaks your heart, but you can't shake your suspicion. You keep seeing your son-in-law around town with a woman whose looks you don't like. Your daughter-in-law leaves the kid at your home when your son is working late.

What's a mother to do with these horrible thoughts? Should she let on to her cheating in-law child that she knows what's going on, nip it before it gets too far? Should she gently mention something to her too-trusting child? Is there anything at all a mother can do?

I'm afraid not. Nine out of ten times, husbands and wives suspect the worst long before you do. Just because they haven't had a screaming, ashtray-throwing showdown yet doesn't mean your child is too innocent or inexperienced to see what's going on. Staying out of this situation is going to be a monumental test of your self-restraint—as a mother *and* as a mother-in-law.

Even in an intolerable relationship, it takes time to gather your strength and reconcile yourself to the end of love. No matter how long it takes, everyone deserves the time to settle these matters alone. Everyone lives by a different emotional clock.

We don't stop loving somebody because they have stopped loving us. Couples break up when one or both members gain the personal strength to say, "Enough. I'm out of here." But hurts can also be forgiven. Sometimes it is possible for a couple to survive the trauma of an affair, especially one that hasn't become public knowledge. Hearts can heal. No mother, or mother in-law, has the right to take that chance away from her child.

When a mother gets intricately involved in her children's marriage problems, it changes the drama in ways even the most well-intentioned person would never dream of. Trying to force your son or daughter into acknowledging what's going on is a recipe for disaster. If your child is in denial, he or she will probably figure you are seeing things that don't exist and perhaps believe you are just causing trouble. If he or she is aware of what's been going on—and has chosen for whatever reason to keep quiet about it—all you've succeeded in doing is humiliating your own child for something that is not his or her fault to begin with. The fact that you know about your son-in-law's or daughter-in-law's infidelity will be crushing news. You won't even necessarily convince your child to do something drastic about it, if that was your plan.

True story: A friend and her husband lived in a rental apartment above her mother's home. The mother was almost positive that her son-in-law was having an affair with the wife of his best friend. She'd overheard some intimate-sounding phone calls between them and seen them out together more than once. The thought of this man fooling around drove the mother into an indignant rage. She could no longer sleep nights. The knowledge was eating her up.

One night, after another of his disappearing acts, her daughter and son-in-law got into another argument. Only this time it was a real window-rattler; the whole block must have heard them. The mother couldn't stand it any longer. She marched upstairs, burst into their apartment, and demanded that her son-in-law leave the house that night.

Stunned silence from her daughter and son-in-law. Was she serious? You bet she was. Because he wasn't moving fast enough, her mother started to help matters along. She threw his clothes down the steps, all the while hollering that he should go stay at his girlfriend's house and never come back.

The daughter had no idea that her mother knew about her husband's indiscretions. Unable to stop the berserk outburst, the daughter could only stand there, shell-shocked, as her husband's clothes and books cascaded down the stairs.

My friend's husband left that night and never returned. Time and time again, she tried to persuade him to move back, but he refused.

"I did you a favor," her mother protested. "You'll thank me for it someday." But no one ever thanked her.

After a time, her mother realized what she'd done to her daughter and her marriage and repented. "What should I have done?" the mother asked. She should have kept her suspicious thoughts and her anger to herself, that's what. If it became truly unbearable, she could have talked with an outsider—a minister, a therapist, a trusted friend. She could have vented her anger and perhaps avoided a lot of unnecessary pain.

As it turned out, she'd accused her son-in-law unjustly. True, he had developed a very close relationship with his best friend's wife. Maybe too close, he admitted, but they'd never been intimate. "We liked spending time together and shared a lot of the same interests," he said. "But it was all very innocent."

He never forgave his wife for standing on the sidelines while her "crackpot mother" (his words) tossed him out. "It's bad enough when your wife throws your clothes all over the yard. But when your mother-in-law does it ... give me a break. My wife just stood there!" he said. "I feel she should have thrown her mother out or come with me when I left. I lost all respect for my wife that night. She had never grown up. She was never a wife—she was still acting like her mother's daughter."

Yes, her mother's motives were pure, and any move to protect one's daughter from harm seems abundantly justified. When we see our children being hurt or simply unappreciated, common sense goes right out the window (or down the stairs). What her mother didn't comprehend is that she had no right to make decisions her daughter would have to live with the rest of her life. No one should have to live with the responsibility of causing what this mother did —a broken marriage and a broken home.

31

When Their Marriage Is Over

WHEN MY ex-husband and I got divorced, it made a wreck out of my mother. He loved my mother to death, catered to her, and took her wherever she wanted to go. Given a choice, I'm positive my mother would have kept my ex-husband and gotten rid of me.

It happens. After many years, a son-in-law or daughter-in-law becomes such an important part of your family structure that divorce hits you as hard as it does your married children. Over time, your in-law children play irreplaceable roles in your family. Is your son-in-law the one member of your family you can always count on to be there for you? Have you always depended on your daughter-in-law to help you sort out your financial affairs? Does your son-in-law run out to the store without a word of complaint to get whatever small thing you forgot to buy? (My ex-husband did.) Does your daughter-in-law always make you laugh? When your married children announce they have decided to split up, what are you supposed to do?

First, you're going to feel awful. You're allowed to, and you're allowed to show it. What you shouldn't do, or show, is that you have taken sides. Stay out of the blame game. You don't belong in it.

You should always be careful when people close to you break the news that their relationship is ending, or even that they are going through a rough time with their partners. Comfort them, let them know how bad you feel, but if you start in on their spouse ("I never liked the way he treated you anyway" or "You should be happy that you don't have to put up with her anymore"), your comforting words may come back to haunt you. What happens when your daughter makes up with her husband after you've told her you always hated the guy? One thoughtless comment at a critical moment, and you could be paying for it for a long time. If it doesn't turn out to be the end after all, where are you then?

Keep in mind that divorce is not the end of the road for you or for your married kids. Unfortunately, it's only the beginning.

Let's say your daughter-in-law has been a full-fledged member of your family and the mother of your grandchildren for years. She has been your friend and you've shared each other's secrets. She knows all your relatives and how you feel about each of them. She was there for you when you had trouble in your own marriage. She's been good to your mother. Your husband thinks the sun rises in her eyes. What do you do when your son announces that he has fallen in love with someone else and is leaving her?

Your heart is broken, and you don't know how to help her ease her pain. Maybe you can begin by asking members of your family to treat her the same way they always have. It's important to show your daughter-in-law that all the love between you is genuine.

I hear it all the time. "I don't miss my ex-husband, but, boy, I sure do miss his family. We used to be so close and now they never call me anymore. It's like I was never in the family in the first place. I thought they really liked me." The experience of loss and abandonment is worse if your daughter-in-law is made to feel she has lost your whole family as well.

If you went shopping with her once a week, don't stop now. Even if she refuses the first few times, ask again. For the first year, at least, invite her to as many of your family affairs as you can. If she decides not to come, that will be her choice.

If your son has a hard time with the idea that you are inviting his ex-wife to a family wedding, reassure him that you are not taking sides. Let him know that you're praying she will find a new life sooner or later. But until your former daughter-in-law can move on, you can't cut all ties with her and pretend she's never been part of your life. All you can hope is that your son understands and makes his peace with what you are trying to do.

Does your daughter-in-law need to talk for hours about how he hurt her? It's now your job to listen. Just listen. No matter how badly you feel for your in-law child, you don't have to knock your own child to be supportive. You're dealing with someone who is angry and depressed. Don't give in to the temptation to share your own tales of parental disappointment.

All children have done awful, frustrating things to their parents over the years. Save those stories for someone else. Your daughter-in-law needs somebody to listen. Find constructive ways to help, but agreeing with your in-law child that your own son is a fish-eyed monster is not one of them.

Also, be careful not to say things that you could regret later. Are you tempted to vow that you'll never let your new daughter-in-law in your house? Or that you'll never set foot in their new apartment?

Saying things like that may be understandable, but you can't afford to let off steam right now. Stay in control, especially around your grieving in-law child. No matter what you think of your son or what he has done to screw up the marriage, you don't have the right to threaten their chance for future happiness.

Face facts. At first, your son's ex may not like that you have accepted her successor. But sooner or later she will see that your love for her does not necessarily mean that you will go out of your way to hurt your own child.

Eventually, you will have to welcome your new daughter-in-law into the family. The first time you go to visit your son and his new wife, your ex-daughter-in-law will see it as betrayal if you promised in a weak moment that you'd never do that. Avoid saying things that could put your back to the wall later on.

If she thinks she'd like to see a counselor or therapist,

offer to drive her there the first time. If she does not have the money—and you do—offer to pay. If she's unsure of herself or nervous, offer to sit in on the first session.

When your ex-daughter-in-law starts getting angry at you, don't take it personally. What's happening is inevitable, especially if she has had no real contact with your son since the breakup. Your ex-daughter-in-law will try to vent her feelings through you. At times, it may seem as if she is striking out at you, but understand that you are just the vehicle. After all, you are the mother and a pretty potent symbol of the person who is the source of the hurt.

Hang in there. This mood will pass too. Throughout this awful separation, many nasty things will be said on both sides and a lot of feelings will be hurt before the dust settles. Don't get caught up in the drama. Your role is offstage.

When the situation is reversed—when it's your daughter who is splitting with your son-in-law—you'll need to handle your son-in-law a little differently.

Men often don't express their feelings very well, and they need to be pushed a little. Invite your son-in-law to make his usual visits. If he says no, it makes him feel funny to come over without his wife, suggest going out to dinner. How about meeting him with your husband for Sunday breakfast at a restaurant?

Make sure the men in your family continue to include him in their plans. If your son-in-law played golf regularly with your sons or husband or went to the ball park or bowling, make sure they don't stop calling him. If he misses a night, call him and tell him you missed him. Ask if everything is all right.

Try to stay in touch with his mother and other family members too. It won't be easy, since your daughter is probably being blamed for all the pain. But you're a big girl, you can take it.

During the holidays, make time to have dinner with your former son-in-law or daughter-in-law. Give them a gift, as you always did. Don't forget their birthdays; take them out to dinner and maybe think about ordering a cake. For your son-in-law, see that your husband is there too. For your daughter-in-law's birthday, bring along your sister, daughter, or friends. Make it a real party.

You're going to have to do some improvising when it comes to when and where you should invite them. Whatever happens, go out of your way to include your in-law child in your life in as many ways as possible.

If your friends and family tell you that you shouldn't be in touch with your in-laws any longer, don't try to justify or explain yourself. Just change the subject. You don't have to talk about this with them. Stay clear of the subject until the situation calms down. If you can't, stay clear of advice-giving relatives altogether.

Just when you think things could not get much worse, your new son-in-law or daughter-in-law will probably let you know they don't like the attention you're still giving the ex. It's pretty natural for the new person in your child's life to feel as if he or she is being compared to a predecessor.

Don't get upset, because that won't last either. You can gently say that you care about them too but you aren't the type to abandon people just because they suddenly seem inconvenient to have around. Sooner or later, your new in-law children should come to respect what you have done.

Eventually, your ex in-law will find a new partner. He or she will make new friends and move on in life. Your relationship will begin to fade; it has to. Sure, you will miss them. But knowing how deeply you feel for them, you will never have to say to yourself, I didn't do the right thing.

Okay, what if you never liked the creep your son or daughter married in the first place? When they announce they are breaking up, it's the moment you've been waiting years for. Lucky you.

You never understood what your child ever saw in this person in the first place and why the marriage didn't come flying apart years ago. Now, it's open season on your ex in-law. Swing away, no holds barred. Let all that pent-up hatred come pouring out like a busted dam. Now that your lousy, ungrateful in-law child is on the last bus out of town, you can start throwing all the rocks you want, right?

I'm afraid not. Your day of reckoning will probably never come, especially if your married children have children of their own.

Let's say you were wise enough to keep your mouth shut during the difficult years your daughter was married. Be smart enough to keep up the good work now that her husband is out of the picture.

Bad-mouthing your departing son-in-law in front of friends and family may be sweet, but getting all those bad feelings off your chest can only hurt your daughter. First of all, if you do it in front of others, it's a terrible invasion of her privacy. Making your daughter's personal troubles public is selfish and unfair. Worse, it may well push your ex-son-in-law into looking for more trouble.

If he was truly as bad as all that, let him ride off into the sunset with your blessing and good riddance. Your daughter may call him all the names she wants to as he leaves. You shouldn't, because it could end up boomeranging. Do all your rejoicing in silence.

Your position in their relationship — even though it's over, it is *still* a relationship — has not changed. Whatever you say will come out sounding (to her) like "I told you so." Your daughter is going through enough pain and anger already. You'll only be making it worse. Comfort them, but there's no need to put the knife into your departing in-law child. Enough people are doing it already.

Even if the breakup is a bad one, make sure you continue to show your in-law child's family their fair share of respect. In most cases, they had nothing to do with whatever soured the marriage. If their family did play a part in it, you now have twice the reason not to tangle with them.

I realize how hard it's going to be to keep from celebrating, especially if their marriage has not been good. If you're having trouble maintaining your composure, here's an idea: Try to remember their wedding day.

It was probably not only a happy memory, but it will remind you that your child went into this marriage eagerly. In fact, there was probably no way to stop them. Do you know what that means? Your in-law child can't be blamed totally for whatever went wrong. They chose each other, and they both must bear some responsibility. Take strength in the fact that it's over and everyone gets to start fresh. It's a new beginning. Move on.

About the Authors

CAMILLE RUSSO is a relationship expert with a counseling practice in Queen's. She was born and raised in Park Slope, Brooklyn, New York. After raising a family, she went back to school in 1990 as a psychology student at Queen's college. In 1991, Camille was asked to intern in a pioneer juvenile-justice program by Manhattan Supreme Court Justice Michael Corriero. As the program's first counselor, she met weekly with the judge to evaluate the teenagers who appeared in his court, and kept track of those who were given alternatives-to-jail sentences in after-school programs, rehabilitation centers, and training programs. This program has been profiled in the *New York Times,* on CNN, *Oprah,* the *Today Show* and CBS's *48 Hours.*

Her work with scores of clients is not psychotherapy as most people know it, but is closer to what business consultants do for corporations. She provides people with expert advice and information to help them solve problems and guide them through troubled times.

MICHAEL SHAIN, her husband, began his newspaper career at the New York Post in 1979 as a television reporter and critic. Over the years, he has written about police and labor stories, food and travel, trials, and the lives of lottery winners.

He wrote a daily gossip column for *New York Newsday* and served as news editor of the respected trade magazine *Mediaweek*.

Shain returned to the *Post* in 1996 to become the paper's media columnist. He has appeared on most of the local New York newscasts and nationally on *CBS Morning, Day and Date, Entertainment Tonight, Inside Edition, Last Call,* and *Charlie Rose.* He is a regular contributor on CNNfn.